Presented to:

_______________________________

From:

_______________________________

Date:

_______________________________

*Pull up a chair. There's always room at the counter.*

# At the Counter

## Spiritual Recipes for Faith in Everyday Life

Laura Sharp-Waites

Manufactured in the United States of America

*This book was written at the counter, one ordinary day at a time .*

# Dedication

This book is dedicated to the women and people who taught me that love often shows up in the kitchen.

To my Great-Grandmother **Maggie**, whose biscuit cabinet still lives in my home. It has held more than flour and bowls; it has held stories, patience, and the quiet wisdom of hands that knew how to make something good out of what was given.

To my grandmother **Nannie**, Maggie's daughter-in-law, who shared her love of cooking, canning, and baking with generosity and joy, teaching me that food is one of the ways we pass love down the line.

To my parents, **Darden & Linda**, thank you for encouraging curiosity, creativity, and courage, especially when it came to trying new things and new recipes. And thank you for giving Todd the butcher block that now rests on Maggie's cabinet, a gift that beautifully connects generations.

And to **Todd**: thank you for setting aside your own projects so mine could come to life, for being my faithful taste tester, my steady encourager, and my biggest supporter. I love you more than words (and maybe even more than cookies).

# Before We Begin

There is no right way to sit at the counter.

You do not need to read this devotional in order. You do not need to finish a chapter each day or arrive with a quiet heart already prepared.

Some days you may read slowly. Other days you may linger over one reflection or simply pause at a prayer.

This book was written for real life, not perfect routines.

Come as you are.

Bring your questions, your weariness, your gratitude, your hunger for something steady.

Pull up a chair.

Stay as long as you need.

# Table of Contents

There is no rush here. No expectation to read perfectly or quickly.

These reflections are meant to be lived with, not finished.

Take a breath. Turn the page when you're ready.

# Introduction

Welcome to the Counter

There is a quiet holiness hidden in ordinary places.

It shows up in kitchens and living rooms, on front porches and in hospital waiting rooms, in the soft hum of early morning and the tired sigh at the end of a long day. It lingers in conversations that wander and in silence that feels companionable. It rests in small acts of care we rarely think to call sacred.

For a long time, I believed faith lived mostly in formal spaces. In sanctuaries. In sermons. In carefully chosen words and sacred rituals. And while those spaces still matter deeply, life taught me something else along the way.

God also dwells at the counter.

At the place where coffee is poured before we are fully awake. Where bread is kneaded while prayers drift upward. Where grief finds a bowl and a spoon and begins to breathe again. Where laughter spills unexpectedly and flour dusts everything in sight.

Somewhere between sermons and cinnamon rolls, hospital visits and chocolate chip cookies, I began to notice that my deepest conversations about faith rarely happened in church pews. They happened here. At the counter. In the middle of life as it actually is.

This book grew out of those moments.

It is not meant to be rushed. It is not meant to impress. It is not meant to fix or solve or hurry anyone along their spiritual journey. Instead, it is an invitation to slow down, pull up a stool, and notice where God is already at work.

This is not a book of polished perfection. It is a place to rest, reflect, and be gently companioned through real life and real faith.

Each chapter is a kind of spiritual recipe card. Some offer reflections. Some offer comfort. Some offer gentle challenges. And some offer actual recipes, the kind that warm kitchens and hearts alike. Together, they form a rhythm of faith rooted in everyday life.

You will find stories from my kitchen and my ministry, moments of humor and honesty, and prayers shaped by both joy and grief. You may also find echoes of your own story along the way. My hope is that these pages become a place where you feel seen, welcomed, and gently reminded that you do not walk alone.

If your life feels busy, this book is permission to pause.
If your heart feels heavy, this book is companionship.
If your faith feels fragile, this book is gentle reassurance.

You do not need to read it in order. You do not need to keep up. You do not need to do anything perfectly. Let the chapters meet you where you are, like a warm mug set quietly beside your hand.

Above all, I hope this book helps you discover what I have come to believe with growing certainty: that God is far more present in our ordinary moments than we often realize.

So come in.
Pull up a stool.
There is space for you here.

# Section I: Beginning at the Counter

Every kitchen has a starting place.

Before the recipes. Before the stories. Before anything is made, there is the moment when someone decides to stay. To sit down. To be present.

This section is an invitation. Not to do more, but to arrive. To notice. To let yourself be where you are.

Nothing needs to be prepared.

There is already room.

# 1

# Pull Up a Stool

"Taste and see that the Lord is
good; blessed is the one who
takes refuge in him."
Psalm 34:8

There's a certain sound a kitchen makes when it's waking up.

The soft clink of a mug against the counter. The hum of the coffee maker. The gentle scrape of a wooden spoon against the side of a bowl. Morning light slipping across flour-dusted countertops. A cat claiming the warmest chair before anyone else has a chance.

This is where my days often begin. Not in a pulpit. Not behind a desk. But here, at the counter.

Maybe your own mornings begin in places just like this.

If you showed up at my house right now, I wouldn't tidy first. I wouldn't apologize for the stack of mail, the half-empty fruit bowl, or the crumb trail that seems to follow baking wherever it goes. I'd just pull out a stool and say, "Come sit."

Maybe you've needed a place like that too.

Because that's how faith usually unfolds. Not in polished moments or carefully curated spaces, but in the middle of ordinary life. In kitchens. At counters. Over coffee. In conversations that wander. In silence that feels safe. In stories that spill out before we realize we needed to tell them.

Pull up a stool.

You don't need to have the right words. You don't need to arrive put together. You don't need to explain yourself.

Just come as you are.

Some days, the counter holds joy. Fresh bread. Warm laughter. Celebration brownies cooling on a rack. Other days, it holds exhaustion, unanswered questions, and soup simmering slowly for someone who needs comfort. Sometimes it holds grief. Sometimes gratitude. Sometimes both, side by side.

This is where I've learned that God is not far away. Not waiting for us to get it right. Not hovering somewhere above the mess. God is here. In the clatter of dishes. In the pause before prayer. In the waiting for dough to rise. In the quiet space between one breath and the next.

The counter has become a kind of altar for me. Not a place of performance, but of presence. A place where life is honest and faith is gentle. A place where I remember that holiness often hides in plain sight.

I don't know what brought you here. Maybe you're tired. Maybe you're hopeful. Maybe you're grieving something you don't yet have words for. Maybe you're simply longing for a slower, kinder way to live your faith.

Wherever you are, there's room.

At this counter, we'll talk about waiting and trust. About weariness and rest. About grief and healing. About joy that surprises us and grace that carries us when we don't think we can take another step. We'll share stories, prayers, and recipes that nourish more than just our bodies.

We'll practice noticing God in small things.

Because faith, like good baking, isn't rushed. It's formed slowly, patiently, lovingly. It rises in its own time. And sometimes, the waiting is where the most beautiful things happen.

So pull up a stool.

Set down whatever you've been carrying.

Take a breath.

You're welcome here.

**Soul Pause**

What does your counter look like right now?

What might it mean to invite God into the ordinary moments of your day?

**Prayer**

God of everyday grace,
meet me in the simple moments.
Open my eyes to your presence
in the ordinary rhythms of my life.
Teach me to linger, to notice,
and to trust that you are already here.
Amen.

# 2

# The Holiness of Ordinary Days

"And whatever you do,
whether in word or deed, do
it all in the name of the Lord
Jesus..." Colossians 3:17

Most days don't announce themselves as holy.

They arrive quietly, dressed in routine. Alarm clocks. To-do lists. Meals to plan. Emails to answer. Laundry that somehow multiplies overnight. The familiar rhythm of getting through one more day.

These are the days we're most tempted to overlook. We move through them quickly, waiting for something more meaningful, more spiritual, more memorable to arrive. We tell ourselves that holiness must belong to special moments. Sundays. Sacred seasons. Milestones marked by ceremony and significance.

But ordinary days make up most of our lives.

And it is here, in the unnoticed middle, that God often chooses to dwell.

I have learned this slowly, standing at the counter, hands busy with simple tasks. Chopping vegetables. Measuring flour. Stirring soup that doesn't need much attention, just time. In these moments, my mind often wanders, and prayers slip in quietly. Not polished prayers. Just honest ones. The kind that sounds more like sighs than sentences.

Sometimes faith looks like lighting a candle before the day begins. Sometimes it looks like feeding yourself something warm when you'd rather skip a meal and keep going. Sometimes it looks like pausing long enough to notice the sunlight on the floor or the smell of bread beginning to bake.

None of it feels particularly spiritual in the moment. And yet, over time, these small practices begin to shape us. They teach us to pay attention. They open our eyes to a God who is already near.

Ordinary days hold grief as well. They are the days when loss settles in quietly, after the phone calls have stopped and the casseroles have been eaten. These are the days when faith feels thin and the work of simply getting out of bed feels heavy. Even here, holiness lingers. Not as easy answers or quick fixes, but as presence. As breath. As the steady promise that we are not abandoned.

I wish I could tell you that every ordinary day feels meaningful, that every moment sparkles with divine clarity. It doesn't. Some days feel dull. Some feel exhausting. Some feel like they disappear as soon as they pass.

But holiness doesn't require our awareness to exist.

God does not wait for us to notice before showing up.

The sacred is woven into the fabric of our days, whether we recognize it or not. It lives in the kindness we offer without fanfare. In the care we extend to ourselves when no one else is watching. In the faithfulness of showing up, again and again, to lives that are rarely dramatic but deeply human.

The counter has taught me this. It holds the repetition of daily life, the sameness we sometimes resent and the rhythms that quietly sustain us. It reminds me that faith is not something we perform for special occasions, but something we practice in small, steady ways.

Perhaps holiness looks like finishing one ordinary day and trusting that God was present in it, even if we never felt particularly inspired.

Perhaps it looks like blessing the day that didn't go as planned.

Perhaps it looks like receiving grace for being human.

If you are waiting for your life to become extraordinary before you believe it matters, let this be your permission to stop waiting. The days you are living now are already sacred ground.

You do not need to escape your ordinary life to find God.
You need only to notice that God is already there.

**Soul Pause**

What makes up most of your ordinary days?

Where might holiness be quietly present, even if you haven't noticed it yet?

**Prayer**

God of the unnoticed and the everyday,
teach me to see the sacred in ordinary moments.
Help me trust that you are present
even when my days feel unremarkable.
Bless the routines, the repetitions,
and the quiet faithfulness of my life.
Amen.

# 3

# When the Kitchen Is Quiet

"He says, 'Be still, and know
that I am God.'"
Psalm 46:10

There are times when the kitchen goes quiet in a way that feels heavier than silence.

Not the peaceful quiet of early morning or the gentle hush after a meal is finished. This is a different kind of quiet. The kind that settles in after something has changed. After voices that once filled the room no longer do. After routines are interrupted. After loss, disappointment, or exhaustion has taken up residence.

The kitchen still looks the same. The counter is still there. The chair is still pulled out. The clock keeps ticking. And yet, everything feels different.

I've stood in that quiet more times than I can count. Sometimes after a long day of ministry, when the words have all been used up. Sometimes after hard conversations that linger long after the dishes are done. Sometimes in seasons when grief presses close and even familiar spaces feel unfamiliar.

In those moments, the quiet can feel uncomfortable. We are not very good at silence. We fill it quickly. We turn on music, scroll our phones, busy our hands, distract our hearts. Silence asks something of us, and we are not always sure we want to give it.

But the quiet has taught me something. It is often where God waits.

Not with answers neatly arranged. Not with explanations or quick comfort. Just with presence. With the steady assurance of being there, even when nothing needs to be said.

When the kitchen is quiet, I notice things I might otherwise miss. The way the light shifts as the day moves on. The soft ticking of the clock. The sound of my own breathing. The weight I've been carrying without naming it.

Sometimes the quiet invites prayer. Sometimes it invites tears. Sometimes it invites nothing more than sitting still long enough to feel what is true.

This kind of quiet does not need to be fixed.

It does not mean something has gone wrong. It often means something tender is happening beneath the surface. A settling. A grieving. A listening.

Faith is not always loud or articulate. Sometimes it looks like staying in the room when silence feels awkward. Sometimes it looks like trusting that God understands the prayers we cannot form.

I have learned that God is just as present in the quiet kitchen as in the busy one. Just as near in the stillness as in the laughter and noise. Perhaps even more so.

If you find yourself in a season of quiet, know this: you are not alone. Silence is not absence. It is often an invitation. An opening. A place where something gentle and honest can begin.

The counter still holds you.
The stool is still there.
God has not stepped away.

Sometimes the most faithful thing we can do is remain present, even when the room is quiet.

**Soul Pause**

When was the last time you noticed a deeper kind of quiet?

What might it be inviting you to hear or feel?

**Prayer**

God of silence and presence,
meet me in the quiet places of my life.
Help me trust that you are near
even when there are no words.
Teach me to listen with patience
and to rest in your steady companionship.
Amen.

# 4

# God in the Simple Things

"Rejoice always, pray
continually, give thanks in all
circumstances..."
1 Thessalonians 5:16–18

Faith often shows up without much fanfare.

Not in grand gestures or dramatic moments, but in the simple, repeated acts that shape our days. Making coffee. Folding laundry. Cooking a meal for someone you love. These are the places where faith quietly takes root, if we let it.

Cast iron biscuits are like that.

When I was little, cast iron was simply how things were cooked. My grandparents used it for nearly everything. Heavy skillets lived on the stove, seasoned by years of use and care. There was no ceremony around it. No explanation. It was just what you reached for when you needed to feed people well.

Those pans carried more than food. They carried routine. Faithfulness. A kind of quiet wisdom that didn't need to announce itself. Meals came together without fuss, and the kitchen felt steady, dependable, safe.

All these years later, cast iron still feels like home.

Todd has quite the cast iron collection now. Skillets in different sizes, well cared for, each with its own personality and history. I like to tease him about it, mostly because I frequently borrow his pans. Sometimes I return them right away. Sometimes they linger on the stove a bit longer than planned. He pretends not to notice, though I'm fairly sure he always does.

There's something grounding about cast iron. It holds heat evenly. It forgives uneven attention. It doesn't mind being used again and again. In many ways, it mirrors the kind of faith I've come to trust. A faith that isn't flashy, but faithful. Not brittle, but durable. Not perfect, but present.

I've made these biscuits for ordinary mornings and unexpected guests. For slow Sundays and busy weeks. For people who needed comfort and for people who simply needed to be fed. There is something holy about that kind of simplicity. About offering what you have, the way you've always done it, trusting that it will be enough.

Simple things teach us important truths.

They remind us that abundance doesn't require extravagance. That nourishment doesn't need to be complicated. That grace often works through what is already within reach.

On days when my faith feels thin, when words fail and prayers feel small, I return to simple practices. I make something warm. I care for the tools that have cared for generations before me. I trust that God is present in the doing, even when I can't quite name what I believe.

Perhaps faith is less about getting everything right and more about showing up to the small things with intention. Perhaps holiness looks like feeding people well. Perhaps God delights in the quiet faithfulness of simple acts done with love.

This is where theology meets the countertop. Where belief becomes embodied. Where grace takes shape in flour and butter and heat.

**From My Counter: A Few Kitchen Notes**

These are small things I've learned over time that make baking a little easier.

**Measuring Flour** I recommend weighing flour with a kitchen scale whenever possible. It gives more consistent results and helps avoid adding too much flour without realizing it. If you don't have a scale, gently spoon flour into your measuring cup and level it off with a knife rather than scooping directly from the bag.

**Making Buttermilk at Home** If you don't have buttermilk on hand, you can make a quick substitute. Add 1 tablespoon of vinegar or lemon juice to 1 cup of milk and let it sit for about 5 minutes until slightly thickened before using.

## Cast Iron Biscuits

These biscuits are sturdy, forgiving, and meant to be shared. They don't ask for perfection. They simply ask to be made, shared, and enjoyed.

**Why These Biscuits Matter**

I think of these as *welcome biscuits*. The kind you make when someone pulls up a stool. When you're not sure what else to offer, but you know food will help. The kind that say, *You belong here*, without needing to say a word.

They carry memory, care, and faith forward, one batch at a time.

## Ingredients

- 2 cups all-purpose flour
- 1 tablespoon baking powder
- 1 teaspoon salt
- 1/4 cup cold butter, cut into small pieces
- 3/4 cup buttermilk

## Instructions

1. Preheat the oven to 425°F. Place your cast iron skillet in the oven while it heats.

2. In a bowl, whisk together flour, baking powder, and salt.

3. Cut in the cold butter until the mixture resembles coarse crumbs.

4. Stir in the buttermilk just until the dough comes together.

5. Carefully remove the hot skillet and lightly grease it.

6. Turn the dough into the skillet and gently pat it into an even layer.

7. Cut the dough into wedges or squares.

8. Bake for 15–18 minutes, until golden on top.

**Soul Note**

As these biscuits bake, notice how ordinary ingredients become something nourishing through heat and time. Let this be a reminder that God often works the same way, shaping faith quietly through daily use and care.

**Soul Pause**

What simple tools or traditions carry meaning for you?

Where might God be present in the ordinary things you reach for each day?

**Prayer**

God of simple gifts,
bless the work of my hands.
Thank you for the faith passed down
through generations,
for the love held in familiar tools,
and for the grace found in ordinary meals.
Meet me here, in the doing.
Amen.

# 5

# Learning to Stay

"Remain in me, as I also
remain in you..." John 15:4

Staying is harder than it looks.

We live in a world that celebrates moving on. New beginnings. Fresh starts. The next thing. We are encouraged to pivot quickly, upgrade often, and leave behind anything that feels uncomfortable, unresolved, or slow.

But faith has a different rhythm.

Faith often asks us to stay.

Stay with a conversation that hasn't resolved yet.
Stay with a silence that feels heavy.
Stay with questions that don't come with immediate answers.
Stay with people whose pain cannot be fixed by words.

Learning to stay doesn't come naturally to most of us. It didn't to me. I've felt the pull to move on, to tidy things up, to offer reassurance before it was ready. Especially in ministry, there is a quiet pressure to *do something*, to say the right thing, to make meaning quickly.

But some moments don't ask to be fixed.
They ask to be held.

There are seasons when my role has been simply to hold tension for others. To sit with people in their uncertainty. To remain present when the silence stretches longer than feels comfortable. To resist the urge to rush them toward resolution or hope before they are ready.

Holding that kind of space is work. Sacred work. It requires patience and trust and a willingness to stay when leaving would be easier.

I've learned this in the kitchen, too. Some things can't be hurried. Dough needs time. Soup needs to simmer. You can't rush the process without losing something essential. You stay nearby, attentive but not anxious, trusting that something is happening even when you can't see it yet.

There have also been moments when staying meant being awakened in the middle of the night.

More than once, I've been stirred from sleep with a name on my heart. No explanation. No details. Just a deep sense that prayer was needed. So I got up, wrapped myself in a blanket, and prayed in the quiet dark. Not eloquent prayers. Just faithful ones. Trusting that God knew what I did not.

Later, I learned that the person I had prayed for needed it at that very moment.

Those experiences have taught me something important about staying. Sometimes staying means listening closely enough to respond when God nudges us awake. Sometimes it means trusting that our presence in prayer matters, even when we don't understand why.

Staying can feel like standing still while the world keeps moving. It can feel unseen. It can feel inefficient. But staying is where so much of life and faith are formed.

I've stayed in ministry when I was tired.
I've stayed in prayer when words felt thin.
I've stayed in silence with others when nothing could be said.

Those were not glamorous seasons. They didn't come with clear markers of success. But they shaped me in ways that movement never could.

Staying taught me that God often does God's deepest work not in moments of action, but in moments of presence. Not when we rush forward, but when we remain open, attentive, and faithful in uncertainty.

Learning to stay doesn't mean ignoring pain or denying the need for change. It means listening carefully before leaving. It means honoring the holy work that can only happen when we remain present long enough for trust to grow.

If you are in a season where staying feels difficult, you are not failing. You are practicing faith in one of its quietest and most demanding forms.

Sometimes staying looks like sitting with someone in silence. Sometimes it looks like getting up to pray in the night. Sometimes it looks like trusting that God is at work beyond what you can see.

You don't have to stay forever.

But perhaps you can stay for today.

And today might be enough.

**Soul Pause**

Where are you being asked to hold space rather than offer answers?

What might it look like to stay present, even when the outcome is unclear?

**Prayer**

God of patience and presence,
teach me the courage of staying.
Help me hold space with tenderness
and trust you in the silence.
Wake me when prayer is needed,
and give me grace for today.
Amen.

# 6

# Flour-Dusted Faith

"My grace is sufficient for you,
for my power is made perfect in
weakness." 2 Corinthians 12:9

Faith is rarely tidy.

It doesn't stay neatly contained within the lines we draw for it. It spills. It clings. It leaves a trace long after the work is done. Much like flour, it has a way of getting everywhere.

Sometimes it even gets on the cat.

More than once, I've looked down and realized that Sassy has a faint dusting of flour on her fur, usually from wandering too close to the counter while I'm baking. She never seems bothered by it. She simply carries on, as if this is exactly what she signed up for.

Faith feels like that to me now.

I used to believe faith should look clean. Orderly. Controlled. I wanted my life, my work, and my calling to reflect competence and excellence at all times.

Somewhere along the way, perfection became the goal, and exhaustion became the cost.

It took me a while to realize that only Jesus is perfect.

Trying to be perfect myself only left me tired, concerned, and constantly measuring whether I had done enough. Faith felt like something to maintain rather than something to live.

These days, I can say with gratitude that I am a recovering perfectionist. I am learning to be comfortable with things undone. With mess. With lives that look lived instead of curated. With faith that carries fingerprints and flour smudges.

One moment stands out as a turning point for me.

During my final project for my Deaconess Program, I created a concrete casting of a large leaf. I did everything carefully. I researched the process, interviewed someone who had experience, gathered all the materials. Todd helped me mix the tinted concrete, and I carefully poured it over the leaf, which was supported underneath by sand.

When we unmolded it, it was beautiful.

Todd suggested setting it upside down so it would not roll off the table. As he gently placed it down, the weight of the base shifted, and the base fell and crushed the edges. The piece shattered into what felt like a million fragments.

In the past, I would have started over. Remade the project. Submitted a flawless version. No one would have known.

This time, I didn't.

Instead, I submitted the broken pieces, just as they were. I shared what had happened. I named the growth. I spoke honestly about how God was using that moment to loosen my grip on perfection and deepen my trust.

It was one of the most painful and faithful things I have ever done.

Flour-dusted faith looks like that. It's the willingness to let what is broken be seen. To trust that authenticity tells a truer story than polish ever could. To believe that God is at work not in spite of the mess, but often right in the middle of it.

Faith that never gets dusty is often faith that never leaves the shelf. But faith that is lived, practiced, and risked will always carry marks of the work it's been doing.

If your faith feels smudged, unfinished, or imperfect, you are not failing. You are living it.

God does not ask us to be flawless.
God invites us to be faithful.

So let the flour fly. Let the edges be uneven. Let the broken pieces tell the truth. Let faith cling to you in small, ordinary ways, even if it shows up on the cat.

Those traces are signs that something real is happening.

**Soul Pause**

Where are you releasing the need to be perfect?

What broken or unfinished places in your life might be telling a deeper story of grace?

**Prayer**

Jesus, perfect in love,
free me from the burden of needing to be flawless.
Teach me to trust you with what is unfinished,
broken, or imperfect in me.
Bless the mess, the learning, and the living.
Amen.

# 7

# Starting with What You Have

"Moses stretched out his hand
over the sea, and all that night
the Lord drove the sea back..."
Exodus 14:21–22

There is a quiet wisdom in beginning where you are.
Not where you wish you were.
Not where you think you should be by now.
But right here, with what is already in your hands.

Starting with what you have requires honesty. It asks us to look at our resources, our energy, our faith, and our lives as they actually are, not as we imagine they ought to be. That can feel vulnerable. Especially if we're used to waiting until things feel more complete, more certain, or more impressive.

But faith rarely begins with abundance.

It begins with willingness.

I've learned this in the kitchen more times than I can count. There are days when I open the pantry and feel uninspired. Nothing feels special. Nothing feels like enough. And yet, when I begin with what's there, something usually comes together. A simple meal. A shared moment. Enough nourishment for the day.

Starting doesn't require everything to be in place. It requires movement. A first step. A small act of trust.

In ministry and in life, I've watched people hesitate because they believe they don't have enough faith, enough clarity, or enough strength to begin. I've felt that hesitation myself. The belief that once things feel more settled, more certain, then we'll be ready.

But readiness often comes *after* we begin.

Scripture tells a similar story.

I think of Moses standing at the edge of the sea, with fear behind him and water in front of him. The path forward was not visible. The danger was real. And still, he lifted the staff God had already placed in his hands. In Exodus 14:21–22, the sea does not part because Moses had a clear plan. It parts because he stepped forward in trust with what he already had.

Faith did not wait for certainty.
It moved first.

Starting with what you have is often like that. You don't begin because the way is clear. You begin because God has nudged you forward, and you trust that movement will make space where none seems possible.

Starting with what you have means trusting that God works through limited resources and imperfect beginnings. It means believing that small offerings matter. That effort counts. That faith doesn't need to be fully formed to be faithful.

There are seasons when starting looks unimpressive. Quiet. Almost invisible. It might be choosing to pray even when words feel thin.

Offering care when your own reserves feel low. Taking one small step when the path ahead feels uncertain.

These beginnings don't always feel brave, but they are.

The counter teaches this lesson well. It holds half-empty bowls and uneven measurements, last-minute substitutions and second tries. It reminds me that good things are often made from ordinary ingredients gathered without ceremony.

You don't have to wait for perfect conditions.
You don't have to gather more than you already have.
You don't have to know how everything will turn out.

Begin where you are.

God will meet you there.

**Soul Pause**

What do you already have that you've been overlooking?

Where might God be inviting you to take a first step, even if the way forward isn't clear yet?

**Prayer**

God who makes a way,
help me trust the gifts already in my hands.
Meet me in small beginnings
and give me courage to move forward
before everything feels certain.
Bless what I offer
and part the waters as you see fit.
Amen.

# Section II: Waiting, Trust, and Slow Miracles

Waiting changes the way we move through the world.

Once we have settled in, once we have stayed long enough to notice the quiet and the mess, we begin to encounter the places where faith asks for patience instead of answers.

This section holds the slow work. The unfinished moments. The prayers that linger.

Nothing here needs to be forced.
God is already at work in the waiting.

# 8

# When the Dough Won't Rise

*"But those who hope in the Lord*
*will renew their strength..."*
*Isaiah 40:31*

There are moments when you follow all the steps and still nothing
happens.

You measure carefully.
You wait the right amount of time.
You cover the bowl and set it somewhere warm.
And then you check... and the dough hasn't risen at all.

It's tempting to assume you've done something wrong.

Maybe the yeast was old.
Maybe the water was too hot or too cold.
Maybe you misread the recipe or rushed the process.

Sometimes those things are true. But sometimes, the dough simply
isn't ready yet.

I've learned this the hard way, standing in my kitchen, staring into
a bowl that looks exactly the same as it did an hour ago. Nothing
has changed on the surface. No visible progress. No reassurance that
anything is happening beneath.

Faith can feel like that too.

There are seasons when we pray and wait and do all the faithful things we know to do, and still nothing seems to move. The answers don't come. The circumstances don't change. The healing feels delayed. The clarity we hoped for doesn't arrive.

When the dough won't rise, the waiting becomes personal.

It's easy to grow discouraged in these moments. To question whether our efforts matter. To wonder if we misunderstood what God was asking of us. To feel foolish for hoping.

But dough doesn't rise on our schedule.
And neither does growth.

Much of what happens in baking is invisible. Yeast works quietly, transforming the dough long before anything looks different. The process cannot be rushed without compromising what is being formed.

Faith often grows the same way.

There have been seasons when I wanted visible progress. Something I could point to and say, *See? God is working.* Instead, I was asked to wait. To trust that something was happening beneath the surface. To remain patient when the outcome was uncertain.

Waiting like that stretches us.

It reveals how quickly we want results. How uncomfortable we are with not knowing. How easily we equate movement with faithfulness.

But waiting is not inactivity.
It is participation in a slower kind of work.

When the dough won't rise, the most faithful thing you can do is often the simplest. Cover the bowl again. Adjust the temperature if needed. And give it more time.

Sometimes faith looks like that too. Continuing to pray. Continuing to show up. Continuing to trust even when nothing looks different yet.

If you are in a season where things feel stalled, where progress feels invisible, take heart. This may not be failure. It may be formation.

God does not abandon the process simply because you cannot see the outcome.

Some of the most important work happens quietly, in the waiting, long before anything looks changed.

**Soul Pause**

Where in your life does it feel like nothing is happening right now?

What might it mean to trust that growth is still taking place beneath the surface?

**Prayer**

God of hidden work,
help me trust the process when I cannot see the results.
Give me patience in the waiting
and courage to believe that you are still at work.
Teach me to rest in your timing,
even when I long for change.
Amen.

# 9

# Waiting on Yeast and God

"Though it linger, wait for it; it
will certainly come and will not
delay." Habakkuk 2:3

Waiting is not passive.

It may look still from the outside, but something is always happening
beneath the surface. Yeast is quietly doing its work, transforming what
it touches, even when nothing looks different yet.

I used to think waiting meant doing nothing. That if I wasn't
moving forward, I was somehow falling behind. But yeast taught me
otherwise. It doesn't hurry. It doesn't announce progress. It works
patiently, steadily, faithfully.

Faith often asks us to do the same.

There are seasons when waiting feels reasonable. We understand why
we must pause. We trust the timing. And then there are seasons when
waiting feels unfair. When we've done all we know to do and are left
with nothing but time and uncertainty.

Waiting on yeast means trusting a process you cannot see. You cover
the bowl, step back, and resist the urge to keep checking. You learn,

sometimes reluctantly, that lifting the towel too often only interrupts the work.

Waiting on God can feel like that.

We pray. We hope. We listen. And then we wait. Not knowing when the answer will come or what it will look like. Not knowing if what we are hoping for will arrive at all.

In those seasons, worship becomes an anchor.

Not worship that demands clarity or resolution. Not worship that pretends everything is fine. But worship that says, *Even here, God is still God.* Worship that rises from trust rather than outcome. Worship that does not rush the ending, but honors the presence of God in the middle.

Sometimes worship in the waiting looks like singing when answers are absent. Sometimes it looks like lighting a candle, whispering a psalm, or simply breathing a prayer that says, *I am still here, and so are You.* Sometimes it looks like standing quietly before God without asking for anything at all.

Worship does not make the waiting shorter.
But it makes it bearable.

Scripture reminds us, *"Wait for the Lord; be strong and take heart and wait for the Lord"* (Psalm 27:14), a quiet assurance that faithfulness is found not in speed or success, but in trusting God enough to remain present.

Yeast does not work faster because we are anxious.
And God does not hurry because we are uncomfortable.

Waiting shapes us.

It teaches us humility. It softens our grip on outcomes. It reminds us that we are not the ones in control. Worship in the waiting keeps our hearts open while that shaping happens. It keeps waiting from turning into despair.

I have waited for clarity that took longer than I wanted. I have waited for healing that came slowly. I have waited for doors to open and for others to close. In those seasons, worship did not remove the uncertainty, but it reminded me who I was waiting *with*.

There is grace in waiting when we stop fighting it.
When we allow ourselves to rest instead of strive.
When we trust that God's timing, though rarely convenient, is always intentional.

If you are waiting right now, waiting for answers, direction, healing, or peace, know this: waiting does not mean nothing is happening. And worship in the waiting is never wasted.

Cover the bowl. Step back.
Lift your heart.
God is faithful in the waiting.

**Soul Pause**

What does worship look like for you when answers are delayed?

How might you remain oriented toward God, even while you wait?

**Prayer**

God of patience and promise,
teach me to worship you in the waiting.
Help me trust your presence
when outcomes remain unclear.
Give me grace to wait without fear
and faith to praise you
before I see what comes next.
Amen.

# 10

# Trusting the Slow Work

*"He who began a good work*
*in you will carry it on to*
*completion..."*
*Philippians 1:6*

There is a particular kind of trust that only grows slowly.

It is not the trust of quick answers or instant reassurance. It is the trust that forms over time, shaped by repetition, patience, and experience. The kind that settles into your bones rather than rushing to your lips.

The slow work asks something different of us.

It asks us to believe that growth is happening even when progress is not obvious. That transformation does not need to announce itself to be real. That God is faithful not only in breakthroughs, but in long stretches of ordinary days.

Baking teaches this lesson well. Some of the best things cannot be hurried. Dough develops flavor slowly. Heat works its way in over time. Rushing the process may produce something edible, but it rarely produces something good.

Faith is formed the same way.

There have been seasons when I wanted clarity quickly. When I wanted God to hurry things along, to make the next step obvious, to bring resolution sooner rather than later. Trusting the slow work felt uncomfortable. Inefficient. Even a little frightening.

But looking back, I can see how much was happening beneath the surface.

The slow work was teaching me to listen more closely. To release my grip on outcomes. To rely less on certainty and more on presence. To notice the small ways God was shaping my heart while I waited for larger answers.

Trusting the slow work means resisting the urge to measure faith by visible results. It means believing that God is not absent simply because nothing dramatic is happening. It means honoring the quiet formation that takes place in unseen places.

Slow work often looks unimpressive from the outside. It rarely earns attention or applause. And yet, it is the work that lasts.

I think of faith like a well-worn recipe, passed down and practiced over time. The kind you don't rush because you know it's worth the wait. The kind that holds memory, care, and trust in every step.

Trusting the slow work does not mean we stop hoping for change. It means we trust God in the process of becoming, even when the timeline is longer than we expected.

If you are in a season that feels slow, where progress is subtle and answers are delayed, know this: slowness is not a sign of failure. It may be a sign that something deep and lasting is being formed.

God is not in a hurry.
And you do not need to be either.

Some of the most faithful work God does in us happens quietly, patiently, over time.

Trust the slow work.

**Soul Pause**

Where do you feel tempted to rush right now?

What might it look like to trust that God is at work, even at a slower pace?

**Prayer**

God of patience and promise,
help me trust the work you are doing in me.
Teach me to release urgency
and rest in your steady faithfulness.
Give me grace to grow slowly,
and courage to believe that this is enough for now.
Amen.

# 11

# The Grace of Unfinished Things

"Because of the Lord's great
love we are not consumed..."
Lamentations 3:22

There is a particular discomfort that comes with unfinished things.

Loose ends.
Half-formed plans.
Conversations that never quite reached resolution.
Dreams that stalled somewhere along the way.

We are taught to admire completion. Finished projects. Clear outcomes. Tidy endings. Unfinished things, on the other hand, can feel like evidence of failure or lack of discipline. Something left undone. Something not quite right.

But life rarely arrives complete.

Most of what we carry is still in process. Still unfolding. Still becoming. And faith, I've learned, is no exception.

I used to believe that faith should feel settled. Certain. Resolved. That unanswered questions or incomplete understanding meant I was doing something wrong. I wanted clarity, closure, and confidence, preferably all at once.

What I've come to see is that unfinished faith is often the most honest kind.

There is grace in the middle. Grace in what is not yet complete. Grace in the places where answers are still forming and stories are still being written.

In the kitchen, unfinished things are everywhere. Dough resting under a towel. Soup simmering longer than expected. Ingredients laid out, waiting to be combined. These moments are not mistakes. They are part of the process. Rushing them would only flatten what needs time to develop.

Faith works the same way.

There are seasons when we live with questions instead of conclusions. When prayer feels ongoing rather than answered. When healing comes in increments instead of all at once. These unfinished places can feel uncomfortable, but they are not empty.

God does not abandon what is incomplete.

I think of all the times Scripture leaves space rather than resolution. Stories that end with waiting. Promises still unfolding. People called faithful long before their lives made full sense. God seems remarkably comfortable working in process.

Unfinished things teach us to trust without having the whole picture. They keep us attentive, open, and dependent. They remind us that faith is not a finished product but a living relationship.

There is grace in allowing something to remain unfinished when it needs more time. Grace in admitting that you don't have it all figured out. Grace in trusting that God is still at work, even when you can't see how the pieces will fit together.

If you are carrying something unfinished right now, a decision, a calling, a relationship, a healing that feels partial, hear this gently: unfinished does not mean forgotten. It does not mean wasted. It does not mean God has stepped away.

It may simply mean that the story is still being told.

You are allowed to live in the middle.
You are allowed to grow without rushing.
You are allowed to trust God with what is not yet complete.

There is grace here.

**Soul Pause**

What feels unfinished in your life right now?

What might it look like to trust God with the process rather than demand completion?

**Prayer**

God of beginnings and becoming,
meet me in the middle of what is unfinished.
Help me trust your work in progress
and release my need for tidy endings.
Give me grace to live faithfully
even when the story is still unfolding.
Amen.

# 12

# Taking a Chance

In their hearts humans
plan their course, but the
Lord establishes their steps."
Proverbs 16:9

Most chances don't announce themselves dramatically.

They arrive quietly, often through someone else. A suggestion. An invitation. A gentle nudge that sounds almost casual. *You should try this. I think you'd like it. There's a challenge going on.*

That's how this one came to me.

A friend named Sherry mentioned a baking challenge and suggested I try making Dutch oven bread. I listened politely. I nodded. And inside, I hesitated. This wasn't how I usually baked. High heat. No kneading. A long, slow rise. Dropping dough into a blazing hot pot felt more like a leap than a recipe.

Still, something about the invitation stayed with me.

Taking a chance rarely begins with confidence. It begins with curiosity. With wondering what might happen if you said yes before you felt fully ready.

When it came time to try, Todd brought me a cast iron Dutch oven that had belonged to my grandmother, Nannie. The pot was heavy, well-seasoned, and familiar in a way that reached deeper than technique. It had already known years of meals, care, and quiet faithfulness. Holding it felt like being handed more than a tool. It felt like being trusted with a story.

That mattered more than I realized at first.

The dough itself was loose and shaggy, nothing like the smooth, controlled textures I was used to. I followed the instructions, covered the bowl, and walked away for hours. There was no shaping to perfect, no kneading to manage. Just waiting and trust.

Then came the heat.

The Dutch oven sat in the oven, growing hotter by the minute. When it was time, I moved quickly, shaping the dough just enough to hold together, lowering it into the pot, and closing the lid. There was no fixing it once it went in. No adjusting. No second-guessing.

I had to let go.

When the lid finally came off, the bread was beautiful. Crackled crust. Deep color. A sound that rang hollow when tapped. I hadn't expected to love it as much as I did.

That's often how taking a chance works.

We imagine risk as something bold or dramatic, but more often it looks like trusting a process you don't fully understand. Like responding to an invitation that stretches you just enough to feel uncertain. Like allowing yourself to try something new while being held by what came before.

That bread rose in a vessel shaped by another generation's faithfulness. I didn't step into the unknown alone. I carried memory with me. I borrowed courage seasoned over time.

Taking a chance is not about being reckless. It's about being responsive. It's about trusting that God can meet us not only in waiting, but also in movement. Not only in staying, but in stepping forward when the time feels right.

I don't believe God asks us to take chances without preparation. The waiting chapters of life matter. The slow work matters. Learning to stay matters. But sometimes, after all that formation, grace opens a door and invites us to walk through.

Not because we are fearless.
But because we are held.

If you feel an invitation stirring in your life, something small but persistent, something that keeps returning to your thoughts, pay attention. It may not be a command. It may simply be an opening.

Taking a chance doesn't guarantee success. But it does open us to joy we might otherwise miss.

Sometimes faith rises not because we waited longer, but because we trusted what had already been placed in our hands.

Not long after that first loaf, my parents gave me an enamel-glazed cast iron Dutch oven for my birthday. A pot meant not for borrowing, but for continuing. For future bread, future chances, future learning. It felt like a quiet blessing, a way of saying, *Keep going.*

Faith often unfolds like that. We begin by borrowing courage, stepping into something new with what has been entrusted to us. And over time, God provides what we need to carry the work forward ourselves.

# Dutch Oven Bread

This bread is about trust. Trusting time. Trusting heat. Trusting that what feels uncertain can still turn out beautifully.

## Ingredients

- 3 to 3½ cups all-purpose flour (375-437.5 grams)

- 1 teaspoon active dry yeast

- 1 teaspoon salt

- 1½ cups water (70°–75°F)

## Directions

1. In a large bowl, whisk 3 cups flour, yeast, and salt. Stir in water and enough remaining flour to form a moist, shaggy dough. Do not knead.

2. Cover and let rise in a cool place until doubled, 7–8 hours.

3. Preheat oven to 450°F. Place a Dutch oven with lid on the center rack and heat for at least 30 minutes.

4. Once the Dutch oven is heated, turn out dough onto a generously floured surface. Using a metal scraper or spatula, quickly shape into a round loaf. Gently place on a piece of parchment.

5. Using a sharp knife, make a ¼-inch-deep slash across the top of the loaf.

6. Using the parchment, immediately lower the bread into the heated Dutch oven. Cover and bake for 30 minutes.

7. Uncover and bake until deep golden brown and the loaf sounds hollow when tapped, 15–20 minutes longer, partially covering if browning too quickly.

8. Remove loaf from pan and cool completely on a wire rack.

**Soul Note**

Some transformations require heat. Some require letting go of control. And some are carried forward by the faith and love of those who came before us.

**Soul Pause**

What invitation keeps returning to you?

What trusted memories or tools might already be supporting your next step?

**Prayer**

God of invitation and inheritance,
thank you for the courage passed down to us
through hands, stories, and love.
Help me trust you when I step into the unfamiliar,
and remind me that I am never walking alone.
Amen.

# Section III - Tending What Is Weary


Eventually, the waiting gives way to weariness.

Not the dramatic kind. The quiet kind that settles into the shoulders and the heart. The kind that comes from showing up faithfully, day after day, carrying more than anyone can see.

This section is about care. About what we need when strength is thin and words feel heavy. About nourishment that restores rather than impresses. About the small, steady ways God tends us through one another.

Here, we make room for rest.
We offer what comforts.
We feed what is tired.

Nothing in this section is rushed.
Nothing needs to be fixed.

This is the place where grace slows down and says, *Let me take care of you now.*

# 13

# When Food Carries Care

*"For I was hungry and you*
*gave me something to eat..."*
*Matthew 25:35*

There are moments when words feel too heavy to carry.

After a surgery.
After a loss.
After a diagnosis.
After the long stretch of days when exhaustion has settled in and conversation takes more energy than anyone has left.

In those moments, food often speaks more clearly than anything else.

When I was serving in a church, chicken pot pie became the meal I returned to again and again. It was something I could carry to a doorstep. Something that reheated gently. Something that didn't demand conversation, but still said, *You are not alone. You are being cared for.*

Pot pie has a way of waiting with people. It sits quietly in the refrigerator until they're ready. It feeds more than one meal. It gathers everyone at the table without asking them to explain themselves.

More often than not, I brought dessert too. A small container of chocolate chip cookies tucked alongside the pot pie. Something familiar. Something sweet. Not because it was necessary, but because it felt kind. Pot pie said, *You are cared for.* Cookies said, *There is still room for comfort.*

I learned quickly that ministry isn't always about saying the right thing. Often, it's about tending what is weary. About showing up with something warm and reliable when words would only get in the way.

This chapter holds two versions of the same meal, because care looks different depending on capacity.

Sometimes you have time and energy, and making something from scratch feels like a gift you're able to offer. Sometimes you don't. And grace means knowing that nourishment still matters, even when shortcuts are necessary.

Both versions are acts of love.

Both say the same thing.

*You matter. You don't have to be strong right now.*

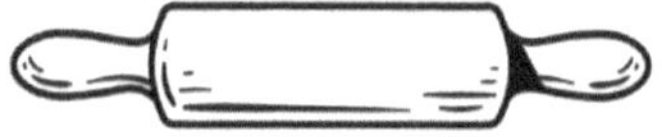

# Laura's Homemade Chicken Pot Pie

*A meal for when you can stay awhile*

**Pie Crust Ingredients *(Makes 2 crusts)***

- 2½ cups all-purpose flour (312.5 grams)

- 1 teaspoon kosher salt

- 6 tablespoons cold unsalted butter

- ¾ cup vegetable shortening, chilled

- ½ cup ice water

**Pie Crust Instructions**

Mix flour and salt in a large mixing bowl. Add ice cubes to a measuring cup and fill with ½ cup cold water; set aside. Grate frozen butter into the bowl or cut into very small pieces. Add chilled shortening and use a pastry blender or fork to cut the fats into the flour until the mixture resembles coarse crumbs.

Add ice water a spoonful at a time, mixing just until the dough begins to come together. Be careful not to overmix, and you may not need all the water. Gently mold dough into a ball.

Divide dough into two pieces and flatten each into a disk. Wrap in plastic and refrigerate for 2 hours (or freeze for 30 minutes).

Roll out dough on a floured surface, starting from the center and rolling outward. Gently transfer to a pie dish, remove parchment, and settle into the pan. Trim and crimp edges.

**Filling Ingredients**

- 1-pound boneless, skinless chicken breasts

- ⅓ cup butter

- ⅓ cup chopped onion

- ⅓ cup all-purpose flour

- ½ teaspoon salt

- ¼ teaspoon freshly ground black pepper

- ¼ teaspoon celery seed

- ½ teaspoon garlic powder

- 1 teaspoon chicken bouillon paste (or more to taste)

- 1 cup milk

- 8 ounces frozen mixed vegetables

- 1 egg

- 1 tablespoon milk

**Filling Instructions**

Season chicken with salt and pepper. Place in a saucepan, cover with water, and simmer until just cooked through. Remove chicken and allow to cool, then chop into bite-size pieces. Reserve 1¾ cups of the cooking water.

Add butter and onion to the saucepan and cook until softened. Stir in flour, salt, pepper, garlic powder, bouillon paste, and celery seed. Slowly add reserved water and milk, stirring until thickened.

Add chicken and vegetables. Taste and adjust seasoning. Allow filling to cool slightly.

Preheat oven to 425°F. Place bottom crust in pie pan, add filling, then top with second crust. Seal edges and cut a small slit in the top crust. Whisk egg and milk and brush lightly over crust.

Bake 40–50 minutes, until golden and bubbly. Cover edges if browning too quickly. Cool 15–20 minutes before serving.

**Make-Ahead & Freezing Notes:**

This pie can be assembled ahead or frozen before or after baking. I often make two at a time, one for dinner and one to freeze for church members after illness or surgery.

# Laura's Shortcut Chicken Pot Pie

*A meal for when you need to show up anyway*

**Ingredients**

- 2 refrigerated unbaked 9-inch pie crusts

- 1 whole rotisserie chicken

- ⅓ cup butter

- ⅓ cup chopped onion

- ⅓ cup all-purpose flour

- Salt and black pepper to taste

- 1¾ cups chicken broth

- ½ cup milk

- 1 (16-ounce) bag frozen mixed vegetables, thawed

- 1 egg

- 1 tablespoon milk

**Directions**

Preheat oven to 425°F. Place one pie crust in a 9-inch pie plate.

Remove skin from rotisserie chicken and shred meat. Melt butter in a saucepan over medium heat. Add onion and cook until tender. Stir in flour, salt, and pepper to form a paste. Add broth and milk, stirring until thickened.

Add chicken and vegetables. Pour mixture into pie plate. Top with second crust, seal edges, and cut a small slit. Brush with egg wash.

Bake 40–50 minutes until golden and bubbly. Let cool 15–20 minutes before serving.

**Soul Note**

Care does not have to be complicated to be holy. God often feeds people through ordinary hands, familiar recipes, and meals that wait patiently until they are needed.

**Soul Pause**

Who might need quiet care right now?

What would it look like to offer nourishment without needing the right words?

**Prayer**

God who feeds us through one another,
bless the meals we carry and the love behind them.
Use what we offer to bring comfort, strength, and rest.
Teach us to show up with grace,
especially when words are few.
Amen.

# 14

# The Kindness of Something Sweet



Not every offering has to be substantial.

Some acts of care arrive small, almost unassuming. They don't fix anything. They don't try to carry the whole weight of the moment. They simply say, *I thought of you.*

That's what dessert does.

When I took chicken pot pie to families after surgeries or during seasons of grief, I usually brought something sweet along with it. Most often, it was chocolate chip cookies. Nothing fancy. Nothing complicated. Just familiar, warm, and kind.

The pot pie did the work of nourishment.
The cookies did something else entirely.

They reminded people that comfort still existed. That pleasure had not disappeared. That joy, even small joy, was still allowed.

Cookies don't ask for much. They don't require conversation or explanation. They can be eaten later, shared quietly, or saved for a moment when the house feels a little too heavy. They carry a gentleness that feels appropriate when words are thin.

I've learned that care is often layered like that. One dish to sustain. One dish to soften. One to meet the body. One to meet the heart.

Chocolate chip cookies have a way of leveling the room. They're familiar across generations. They remind people of kitchens they once felt safe in, of hands that baked for them long ago, of moments when life felt simpler, even if just for a moment.

They don't pretend that everything is okay.
They simply offer sweetness without expectation.

There is something quietly holy about that.

We sometimes think faith must always be serious to be sincere. That joy should wait its turn until the hard parts are finished. But God does not withhold kindness until grief is resolved. God offers it alongside the sorrow, in ways that are gentle enough to receive.

A cookie cannot heal loss.
But it can sit beside it.

If you are caring for someone right now, or if you are learning to care for yourself, remember this: small kindnesses matter. Familiar comforts matter. Sweetness still belongs, even in hard seasons.

Sometimes the most faithful thing you can do is offer something warm, ordinary, and good, and trust that God will use it to remind someone they are still seen.

**Chocolate Chip Cookies**

These cookies are soft, familiar, and meant to be shared. They are not elaborate. They are reliable, comforting, and kind.

## Soul Note

Joy does not betray grief. Kindness does not minimize pain. God often meets us through simple pleasures that remind us we are still held.

## Soul Pause

Where might a small kindness bring light right now?

What sweetness do you need permission to receive?

## Prayer

God of comfort and delight,
thank you for the small joys that carry us
when life feels heavy.
Help me offer kindness freely
and receive it without guilt.
Amen.

# 15

# Grace You Can Pull from the Freezer

*"The plans of the diligent lead*
*to profit as surely as haste leads*
*to poverty." Proverbs 21:5*

Some kindness needs to be ready before you know you'll need it.

That's one of the things life has taught me. Care rarely arrives on a schedule. The call comes late. The text comes suddenly. A hard day stretches longer than expected. And when it does, having something already prepared can feel like mercy.

That's why I love keeping cookie dough in the freezer.

These chocolate chip cookies are thick, chewy, and deeply familiar. They're the kind of cookies people recognize instantly, the kind that feel like home even when you're standing in someone else's kitchen. They're also practical. I can pull out two or twelve, depending on what the moment calls for.

There's something freeing about that.

Care doesn't always need to be made from scratch in the moment. Sometimes the most faithful thing you can do is prepare ahead, trusting that God will let you know when it's time to bake.

I've taken these cookies alongside chicken pot pie. I've baked them late at night after a long day. I've pulled them from the freezer when joy felt thin and sweetness felt necessary. They don't solve anything, but they soften the edges of hard moments in a way that feels kind.

Freezer grace is like that.

It doesn't demand energy you don't have. It waits patiently until it's needed. It reminds you that care can be planned without being impersonal, and that love can be both thoughtful and efficient.

These cookies are generous by design. They make a lot, and that's intentional. Life asks us to show up in ways we don't always anticipate. Having something ready makes it easier to say yes.

And there's grace in that, too.

## Amazing Chocolate Chip Cookies

*Super thick, chewy, and ready when you are*

### Ingredients

- 2 sticks butter, cold (I use salted, but unsalted works too)

- 2 cups brown sugar

- 1 teaspoon almond extract

- 1 teaspoon vanilla extract

- 2 large eggs, cold

- Pinch of salt (omit if using salted butter)

- 3½ cups all-purpose flour (460 grams)

- 4 tablespoons cornstarch

- 1 teaspoon baking soda

- 1 teaspoon baking powder

- 2 cups milk chocolate chips

- 2 cups white chocolate chips

## Instructions

1. In a large mixing bowl, combine the cold butter and brown sugar. Using an electric mixer, beat until well combined.

2. Add almond extract, vanilla extract, and cold eggs. Beat just until incorporated, being careful not to overmix.

3. Add flour, cornstarch, baking soda, baking powder, and a pinch of salt (if using unsalted butter). Mix on low speed until a soft dough forms.

4. Stir in milk chocolate and white chocolate chips until evenly distributed.

5. Using a cookie scoop or spoon, drop dough by heaping tablespoons. I like to roll them into balls.

6. Place dough balls on parchment paper and freeze for at least two hours. Once frozen, store in large Ziploc bags.

7. Preheat oven to 350°F (traditional) or 320°F (convection). Line baking tray with parchment paper.

8. Bake cookies straight from the freezer for 14–16 minutes,

until golden brown.

>    9. Allow cookies to cool completely on the baking tray to firm up. Best served slightly warm.

## Soul Note

Preparing ahead is not a lack of faith. It's an act of wisdom. God often meets us through what we've quietly prepared for moments we didn't see coming.

## Soul Pause

What might it look like to prepare kindness ahead of time?

Where could freezer grace make showing up a little easier?

## Prayer

God of provision and foresight,
thank you for the ways you help us prepare
for moments we cannot yet see.
Bless the care we store up
and the love we offer when it's time.
Amen.

# 16

# When the Table Is Full

*"Share with the Lord's people
who are in need. Practice
hospitality." Romans 12:13*

There is a quiet shift that happens when the table fills.

Not just with food, but with people.
With presence.
With the sounds of forks and small conversation.
With the ordinary grace of sitting together without an agenda.

After seasons of weariness, this kind of gathering can feel tender. Sometimes even awkward. We may not know what to say. We may still be tired. But something in us knows that being together matters.

I've learned that healing doesn't always arrive in solitude. Often, it comes slowly, through shared space. Through meals that stretch a little longer than planned. Through laughter that surprises us. Through silence that doesn't feel heavy because no one is rushing it away.

A full table doesn't mean everything is resolved. It simply means we are not alone.

In the kitchen, I notice how meals change when they're meant to be shared. Portions grow. Recipes become more forgiving. There's less concern about perfection and more attention to making sure there's enough. Enough food. Enough chairs. Enough room for people to arrive as they are.

This kind of hospitality isn't performative. It's relational. It doesn't ask anyone to bring their best self. It asks them to bring themselves.

There have been many tables in my life like this. Tables where grief sat beside gratitude. Tables where joy returned quietly. Tables where no one pretended things were easy, but everyone stayed anyway.

Those tables taught me something important about God.

God is not intimidated by full tables. By noise. By mess. By unfinished stories. God shows up there gladly, inhabiting the ordinary holiness of shared life.

Sometimes restoration looks like rest.
Sometimes it looks like nourishment.
And sometimes it looks like pulling up a chair.

If you are emerging from a hard season, you don't have to rush back to celebration. You don't have to host a feast or find the right words. You can begin by sharing space. By accepting an invitation. By letting yourself be fed in more ways than one.

A full table doesn't solve everything.
But it reminds us that life is still happening.
And that can be enough for today.

**Soul Pause**

Where have you experienced quiet healing through shared presence?

Who might you invite, or accept an invitation from, in this season?

**Prayer**

God who gathers us,
thank you for the tables that hold us
when words are few and hearts are tired.
Help me make room for presence,
and teach me to receive it with grace.
Amen.

# 17

# The Kindness of Soft Things

"He tends his flock like a
shepherd... he gently leads
those that have young."
Isaiah 40:11

There are seasons when strength is not the goal.

Survival is.

During chemotherapy after breast cancer, my body had very clear opinions about what it could and could not tolerate. Foods I once loved suddenly felt impossible. Smells were overwhelming. Textures mattered. And complicated meals were simply too much.

Potatoes became my constant companion.

I ate them in every form I could manage. French fries. Hash browns. Mashed potatoes. Baked potatoes. They were simple, reliable, and gentle. They didn't ask much of me. They showed up quietly and did what they were meant to do.

Potato soup became part of that care.

It was soft. Warm. Nourishing without being demanding. It could be eaten slowly. It didn't require explanation or effort. In a season when my body was doing hard, unseen work, potato soup felt like kindness.

I've learned since then that softness is not weakness.

We live in a culture that praises toughness and resilience, but there are moments when the most faithful response is gentleness. When the body needs food that won't fight back. When the soul needs comfort that doesn't ask for conversation.

Potato soup understands this.

It doesn't rush you.
It doesn't require a strong appetite.
It doesn't insist that you be okay.

It simply offers nourishment.

This is the kind of food I make when someone is worn down. When illness lingers. When grief is still raw. When strength hasn't returned yet. It's the meal that says, *You don't have to push yourself today.*

Even now, I make this soup with care, knowing how deeply food and healing are intertwined. I leave the bacon off because of my pork allergy, but the soup doesn't suffer for it. It's still rich. Still satisfying. Still enough.

That, too, feels like grace.

If you are in a season where your body or spirit feels fragile, let yourself reach for soft things. Food that comforts. Rhythms that slow you down. Care that meets you where you are, not where you think you should be.

God is not disappointed by your need for gentleness.

Sometimes healing begins with a spoon.

# Hearty Comfort Potato Soup

*A soft meal for tired days*

## Ingredients

- 8 potatoes, diced

- 4 cans chicken broth

- 2 cups cold water

- 1 small onion, diced

- 1 teaspoon salt

- 1 teaspoon fresh coarse ground black pepper

- A pinch of celery salt

- 1 cup butter

- ¾ cup all-purpose flour

- 1½ cups heavy cream

## Toppings (Optional, but highly recommended)

- 1½ cups Colby Monterey Jack cheese, shredded

- 1 cup sour cream

- ¼ cup bacon, cooked and crumbled (optional)

- ¼ cup green onion, finely diced

*(I omit bacon due to a pork allergy, and the soup is still wonderfully rich and comforting.)*

**Instructions**

1. Bring water to a boil in a large pot over high heat. Add potatoes and boil until fork-tender, about 10–15 minutes. Drain and set aside.

2. Add chicken broth, water, onions, salt, pepper, and celery salt to the pot. Simmer on low heat for 20 minutes.

3. In a small saucepan, melt butter over low heat. Stir in flour until a paste forms.

4. Gradually add the paste to the soup, stirring constantly, until thickened.

5. Slowly stir in heavy cream. Simmer for 20 minutes, then add potatoes.

6. Serve as is or topped with cheese, sour cream, green onions, or bacon if desired.

**Soul Note**

Gentleness is not giving up. It is wisdom. God meets us not only in strength, but in the care that allows strength to return.

**Soul Pause**

Where do you need softness right now?

What would it look like to let yourself receive gentle care without apology?

**Prayer**

God of healing and mercy,
thank you for the quiet kindnesses
that carry us through hard seasons.
Help me honor my body and my limits,
and trust you in the slow work of restoration.
Amen.

# 18

# When Strength Begins to Return

"Weeping may stay for the
night, but rejoicing comes in
the morning." Psalm 30:5

There is a moment when you realize you're not quite as tired as you
were yesterday.

Not strong. Not finished. Just a little steadier. A little more present.
The fog lifts enough to notice hunger again, not just the need to eat,
but the desire to be nourished.

That's when chicken and noodles show up.

This is not the soup of crisis. It's the soup of recovery. The kind that
signals a turning point. The meal you make when someone is still
healing, but beginning to come back to themselves.

Chicken and noodles carry familiarity. Whenever we visit my parents,
we stop at the Amish store and stock up on angel hair egg noodles.
We bring home several packages and keep them tucked away for illness
or a quick supper on a cold night. It's become part of our rhythm, a
small way of preparing for days when comfort will matter more than
creativity.

Having those noodles on hand feels like a quiet kindness offered ahead of time. They feel reliable. They say, *You've been here before, and you made it through.* They don't demand much, but they offer substance. Protein. Warmth. Something to chew gently, something to finish a bowl of without effort.

I've made this dish when illness started to loosen its grip. When appetite returned slowly. When routine felt possible again, even if energy was still limited. It's a meal that respects the in-between space, not rushing strength, but welcoming it.

This is food for rebuilding.

The broth is steady. The noodles are tender. The chicken is shredded small, already doing the work of being manageable. Everything about it says, *Take your time.*

Chicken and noodles don't pretend that healing is complete. They simply accompany it.

In life, we often want clear markers. A finish line. A declaration that the hard part is over. But restoration is rarely that clean. More often, it comes quietly, through meals like this one, through days that feel a little more doable than the last.

If you are in a season where you are not who you were before, but no longer who you were at your weakest, this meal belongs to you. It honors progress without pressure. It meets you where you are, with warmth and patience.

Strength doesn't always return with celebration.

Sometimes it returns with a bowl and a spoon.

# Chicken and Noodles

*A steady meal for the in-between*

## Ingredients

- 3–4 pounds chicken breast *(My family prefers white meat, but use what your family likes.)*

- 8 cups chicken broth

- 1 large onion, quartered

- 2 cloves garlic, minced

- 1 bay leaf

- 1 teaspoon salt, or to taste

- ½ teaspoon black pepper

- 1 teaspoon celery salt

- 1 teaspoon dried thyme (or 2 teaspoons fresh thyme)

- 2 teaspoons dried parsley

- 12 ounces Amish-style egg noodles *(We like the thin angel hair style, but thicker noodles work too.)*

## Instructions

1. Place chicken in a large pot and cover with chicken broth. Add onion, garlic, bay leaf, salt, and pepper. Bring to a

boil, then reduce heat and simmer for 45–60 minutes, until chicken is tender and fully cooked.

2. Remove chicken and set aside to cool. Strain the broth to remove onion and bay leaf; return broth to the pot.

3. Once chicken is cool enough to handle, shred into bite-sized pieces, discarding skin and bones. Bring broth to a gentle simmer and add celery salt, thyme, and parsley.

4. Add egg noodles and cook until tender, according to package directions. Add additional broth or water if needed to keep noodles covered.

5. Stir shredded chicken back into the pot. Adjust seasoning as needed.

6. Ladle into bowls and serve warm.

## Soul Note

Healing does not erase what came before it. It builds upon it. God meets us not only in our weakest moments, but also in the slow return of strength.

## Soul Pause

Where are you noticing small signs of restoration in your life?

What would it look like to honor progress without rushing what comes next?

**Prayer**

God of healing and hope,
thank you for the ways you restore us gently.
Help me recognize the small signs of strength returning
and trust you in the ongoing work of renewal.
Give me patience for the in-between
and gratitude for each step forward.
Amen.

# 19

# When the Kitchen Comes Back to Life

"There is a time for everything,
and a season for every
activity under the heavens."
Ecclesiastes 3:1

At first, it's almost imperceptible.

The kitchen doesn't burst back into life all at once.

There's no announcement that the hard season has ended. Instead, there are small signs. A pan pulled from the cabinet without effort. A recipe remembered without looking. The quiet realization that you're cooking because you want to, not because you have to.

This is how rhythm returns.

After illness, grief, exhaustion, or long waiting, routine can feel fragile. You may wonder whether you're allowed to settle back into ordinary days. Whether returning to familiar tasks means you've forgotten what was hard. Whether joy has come back too quickly.

But rhythm is not denial.
It is grace finding its way into the everyday again.

When the kitchen comes back to life, it doesn't mean everything is fixed. It means you are present. It means your body and spirit are beginning to trust the day ahead. It means you are learning how to live again without rushing past what shaped you.

I've noticed that when rhythm returns, the kitchen sounds different. There's less urgency. Less proving. Movements are slower, more intentional. You know when to rest and when to stir. You know when something can wait.

This is not the productivity of before.
It is a gentler way of being.

God works deeply in seasons of interruption, but God also delights in our return to the ordinary. The sacred does not disappear when life feels more stable. It settles into the background, woven into habit and practice and quiet faithfulness.

If you're in this season, let yourself receive it.

Cook something familiar. Light a candle. Wash the dishes without rushing. Let the rhythm of the kitchen remind you that life is not only survived. It is lived.

And lived slowly, it can be holy.

**Soul Note**

Returning to routine is not forgetting the hard season. It is honoring what carried you through it

---

**Soul Pause**

What small rhythm is returning to your life right now?

How might you welcome it without pressure or expectation?

---

**Prayer**

God of seasons and steady grace,
thank you for the quiet return of ordinary days.
Help me receive rhythm as a gift,
and trust you in the slow rebuilding of life.
Amen.

# 20

# Learning to Give Thanks Slowly

"Praise the Lord, my soul, and
forget not all his benefits."
Psalm 103:2

Gratitude doesn't always arrive with enthusiasm.

Sometimes it comes softly, almost hesitantly, as we realize something has shifted.

We're not where we once were, but we're also no longer where we were at our weakest. Life has begun to open again, just enough to notice what has returned.

This is the kind of gratitude that grows slowly.

It doesn't list everything at once. It doesn't rush to make meaning. It simply notices. *I can stand here again. I can cook this meal without effort. I laughed today and didn't feel guilty afterward.*

Slow gratitude doesn't deny what was lost. It doesn't erase the hard season or pretend it didn't shape us. Instead, it learns how to hold both truth and thanks in the same breath.

I've learned that gratitude matures with us. Early on, it can feel forced, like something we should feel because others expect it. But later, it becomes quieter and more honest. It rises not from obligation, but from awareness.

This kind of gratitude pays attention.

It notices strength returning without demanding it hurry. It gives thanks for ordinary capacities. It acknowledges progress without insisting on celebration. It understands that being thankful doesn't mean being finished.

In the kitchen, slow gratitude looks like this: recognizing the comfort of familiar tools, appreciating the steadiness of a recipe you know by heart, giving thanks for the simple fact that you're here again, tending life in small ways.

God does not require loud praise to be pleased. God receives whispered thanks just as gladly. Gratitude offered gently is still gratitude.

If you're learning how to be thankful again, let yourself take your time. Gratitude doesn't need to be complete to be faithful. It only needs to be true.

And sometimes, true gratitude begins with one small sentence: *Thank you for this moment.*

**Soul Note**

Gratitude is not a finish line. It is a way of noticing what grace has quietly restored.

**Soul Pause**

What is one small thing you can give thanks for today without needing to explain or expand it?

Where might gratitude be inviting you to slow down rather than speed up?

**Prayer**

God of patient mercy,
thank you for the quiet ways you restore what was worn down.
Teach me to notice your gifts without rushing
past them.
Help me give thanks slowly, honestly, and without pressure.
Amen.

# 21

# Glorified Brownies and the Joy We Inherit

"Go, eat your food with
gladness, and drink your wine
with a joyful heart, for God
has already approved what you
do." Ecclesiastes 9:7

Some joy comes wrapped in memory.

Before I ever knew what a "naked" or plain brownie was, there were Glorified Brownies. Brownies topped with ooey gooey marshmallows and covered in rich chocolate frosting. Brownies that showed up at church functions and family gatherings. Brownies that, to me, simply defined what a brownie *was*.

My grandmother, Mabel, whom I called Nannie, made them faithfully. They weren't fancy. They weren't experimental. They were expected. And loved.

I still remember the shock of discovering a naked brownie for the first time at a third-grade sleepover. I was genuinely confused. Where were the marshmallows? Where was the frosting? Why would anyone stop halfway through something so clearly meant to be finished?

It turns out, some joys are learned early and stay with us.

Glorified Brownies are celebration brownies. They don't whisper. They don't pretend to be subtle. They show up knowing exactly what they are. They are the kind of dessert that assumes abundance, that expects to be shared, that understands there will be enough for everyone.

There is something deeply faithful about that kind of joy.

Not all celebration needs to be earned. Not all sweetness has to be justified. Sometimes joy is simply inherited, passed down through recipes and repetition and the quiet assurance that this, too, is good.

In the life of faith, we often learn restraint before we learn delight. We learn how to endure long before we learn how to celebrate again. But gratitude, when tended gently, eventually gives way to joy that feels safe enough to express itself fully.

Glorified Brownies belong to that moment.

They are joy that remembers.
Joy that gathers.

Joy that doesn't forget the generations that taught us how to celebrate.

If you are in a season where laughter is returning, even tentatively, let yourself receive it. If joy feels surprising, let it stay anyway. God is not offended by sweetness. God delights in it.

Sometimes the most faithful thing you can do is make the brownies your grandmother always made and trust that joy, like grace, is meant to be shared.

# Nannie's Glorified Brownies

*Mabel Eargle (Laura's grandmother, "Nannie")*

**Brownies**

- 1 stick butter, melted

- 1 cup sugar

- 4 tablespoons cocoa

- 2 eggs

- ⅔ cup plain flour

- 1 teaspoon vanilla

- ½ bag chocolate chunks *(chocolate chips work, but chunks are better!)*

- 1/2 bag miniature marshmallows

**Icing**

- 2 cups confectioners' sugar

- ¼ cup cocoa

- 2 tablespoons butter

- 4 tablespoons cream or milk

- 1 teaspoon vanilla

Mix icing ingredients and slowly heat until completely melted and blended. Set aside.

**Directions**

1. Mix brownie ingredients in the order given.

2. Pour batter into a slightly greased 8×8 baking pan.

3. Bake at 350°F for 20 minutes.

4. Two minutes before brownies are done, add a layer of miniature marshmallows (about half a bag).

5. Return to oven until marshmallows melt, about 3 minutes. Do not brown.

6. Remove from oven and immediately pour warm icing over the top.

7. Allow to cool before cutting into squares.

*(Double recipe for a 9×13 pan)*

## Shortcut Glorified Brownies

- 1 box Ghirardelli Triple Chocolate Brownie Mix*(If unavailable, use regular mix and add chocolate chunks or chips)*

- ¼ cup milk

- ¼ cup melted butter

- 2 eggs

- 1 teaspoon vanilla extract

- 1/2 bag miniature marshmallows

- 1 tub Hershey's Frosting *(2 tubs if doubling recipe)*

Prepare brownie mix according to box directions, substituting milk and butter as listed. Bake as directed. Two minutes before brownies are done, add a layer of miniature marshmallows. Return to oven until melted, **not browned**. Cool, then frost with chocolate frosting.

*(Double recipe for a 9×13 pan)*

## Soul Note

Joy passed down is still joy. Celebration remembered is still celebration. God's goodness often arrives through the hands of those who loved us first.

## Soul Pause

What joy did you inherit without realizing it?

Where might celebration be inviting you to show up fully again?

**Prayer**

God of gladness and memory,
thank you for the joys that shape us early
and stay with us through the years.
Help me receive celebration without guilt
and share sweetness freely.
Amen.

# 22

# When Joy Is Better Shared

"Rejoice with those who
rejoice; mourn with those who
mourn."
Romans 12:15

Some joy needs witnesses.

It's one thing to feel joy quietly, tucked into a moment you notice on your own. It's another thing entirely to share it. To bring it into a room. To let it be seen, multiplied, and carried by others.

This kind of joy doesn't arrive all at once. It often follows seasons of restraint, when celebration felt premature or even unsafe. When you learned to hold joy carefully, unsure whether it would last.

But eventually, gratitude matures into something that wants company.

I've noticed that shared joy doesn't need spectacle. It doesn't require a reason that can be explained neatly. Often it shows up in familiar places: church halls, kitchen tables, potlucks where recipes repeat and stories overlap, gatherings where no one is trying to impress anyone else.

There is a particular kind of joy that belongs to communities who have walked through hard things together. It carries memory. It holds tenderness. It knows how to make room for those who are still finding their footing.

Shared joy understands that not everyone arrives at the same place at the same time.

At church functions, celebrations are rarely pure happiness. Someone is always grieving. Someone is always healing. Someone is always holding both joy and loss in the same hands. And still, the table is set. Still, food is passed. Still, laughter finds its way in.

This is not denial.
This is faith practiced together.

Joy that is shared becomes gentler. It learns how to wait. It notices who needs a quieter seat. It leaves room for tears without insisting they disappear.

God's invitation is not just to personal joy, but to communal life where rejoicing and mourning are both welcome. Where no one is asked to match the room's emotional temperature. Where belonging matters more than uniformity.

If joy is returning in your life, consider who might share it with you. Not to perform it. Not to prove anything. Simply to let it grow in the open air of relationship.

Joy, like bread, is meant to be broken and passed.

**Soul Note**

Shared joy does not erase sorrow. It makes room for it and stays anyway.

**Soul Pause**

Who has shared joy with you in a season when it felt fragile?

Where might God be inviting you to let joy be seen, even gently?

**Prayer**

God who gathers us together,
thank you for joy that grows in community.
Help me rejoice without forgetting those who are still hurting,
and teach me to make room for both laughter and tears.
Amen.

# 23

# A Blessing You Can Carry

"The Lord bless you and keep
you; the Lord make his face
shine on you and be gracious
to you; the Lord turn his
face toward you and give you
peace." Numbers 6:24–26

Every gathering needs a blessing.

Not an ending that closes the door, but a word that goes with you. Something you can carry into the next ordinary moment. Something that doesn't rush you forward, but reminds you that you are already held.

That's what this chapter is.

After rhythm has returned, after gratitude has found its footing, after joy has been remembered and shared, what remains is not a command or a conclusion. What remains is presence.

Blessing is not a reward for having done faith well. It is not something earned by endurance or growth. Blessing is simply God's steady regard, offered freely and without condition.

I've come to believe that blessing is one of the most practical gifts we give one another. It doesn't fix anything. It doesn't explain suffering. It doesn't promise ease. It simply says, *You are seen, and you are not alone as you go.*

In kitchens and church halls, around tables and counters, I've watched blessing take shape in small ways. A hand on a shoulder. Food pressed into someone's hands for later. A quiet prayer spoken at the door. These moments rarely feel dramatic, but they linger.

This book has been an invitation to stay. To tend what is weary. To notice grace in ordinary places. To receive joy when it returns and share it when it's ready.

Now the invitation widens. Carry this with you:

- into your cooking

- into your caring

- into your waiting

- into your joy

You do not have to get everything right.
You do not have to hold everything together.
You do not have to rush ahead.

The God who met you at the counter goes with you into whatever comes next.

May you be blessed in the making and the resting.
May you be kept in the ordinary days.
May grace meet you again and again, right where you are.

**Soul Note**

Blessing is not an ending. It is a way of going.

**Soul Pause**

What blessing have you carried with you through a hard season?

Who might need a quiet word of blessing from you this week?

**Prayer**

God of abiding grace,
thank you for walking with us through every season.
As we go,
help us carry your peace into ordinary days.
Bless our coming and our going,
and meet us again where life unfolds.
Amen.

# Section IV - Still Coming Back to the Counter

There comes a point when faith is no longer about getting through something.

The hard season has passed. The sharp edges have softened. Life has settled into something recognizable again. Not perfect. Not uncomplicated. But livable.

This is where most of life happens.

Section IV is for the long middle. The ordinary weeks. The days that don't announce themselves. The Tuesdays and Thursdays when nothing dramatic is unfolding, but faith still needs tending.

You will not find new instructions here. You will find permission.

Permission to return to the counter again and again.
Permission to live your faith without urgency.
Permission to trust that God is still at work in routines, habits, meals, conversations, and quiet persistence.

This section is not about arriving anywhere new. It is about learning how to stay faithful where you already are.

Some weeks will feel light. Others may surprise you with old grief resurfacing or new questions forming. Ordinary time does not mean easy time. It simply means life continues, and God continues with it.

The devotions ahead are meant to be companions.
They do not build toward a climax.
They circle back.
They repeat themes.
They notice seasons changing and rhythms shifting.
They honor the truth that faith is not linear.

You may skip weeks. You may linger. You may return to earlier chapters when you need grounding. That is not misuse. That is how devotional life works.

Still coming back to the counter means you trust that grace is not exhausted by repetition. It means you believe God is patient with your pace. It means you know that showing up again is enough.

As you move through the rest of this book, let the counter remain what it has been all along: a place to pause, to tend what's needed, and to begin again without fanfare.

There is no finish line here.

Only faithfulness, lived one ordinary week at a time.

**A Gentle Word Before You Continue**

You do not have to read these weeks in order.
You do not have to read one each week perfectly.
You do not have to remember everything.

Come as you are. Return when you need to. The counter will still be here.

# 24

# Ordinary Weeks Still Matter

"Who dares despise the day of
small things" Zechariah 4:10

Most weeks are not remarkable.

They don't come with clarity or crisis. They aren't marked by big decisions or visible growth. They simply arrive, one after another, carrying the familiar weight of work, meals, relationships, and responsibilities.

These are the weeks that quietly shape us.

In seasons of intensity, faith can feel dramatic. We pray with urgency. We pay close attention. We mark time by milestones and moments of survival. But in ordinary weeks, faith settles into something quieter. Less noticeable. More woven into the background of daily life.

And that can make us wonder if it still counts.

It does.

Ordinary weeks matter because they are where trust is practiced without fanfare. Where prayer becomes habitual rather than desperate. Where showing up becomes the work itself.

At the counter, ordinary weeks look like routine. Making the same coffee. Washing the same dishes. Reaching for familiar ingredients. There is comfort in this repetition, even when it feels unremarkable. Repetition is not stagnation. It is formation.

God does not withdraw when life feels plain. God delights in steady faithfulness, in small acts of care repeated over time. Scripture reminds us not to despise small beginnings, but it also invites us not to overlook small continuations.

You may not feel inspired this week. You may not feel particularly close to God. You may feel tired, distracted, or simply neutral. None of that disqualifies you from faithfulness.

Faith lived over the long middle of life is rarely exciting. It is dependable. It is patient. It learns how to trust without needing proof every day.

If this is an ordinary week for you, receive it as such. Cook a simple meal. Say a short prayer. Do what is in front of you. Let faith be enough without asking it to be impressive.

God is not waiting for a better version of your week to meet you.

God is already here.

**Soul Note**

Faith is often formed in weeks we would otherwise forget. God does not overlook them.

**Soul Pause**

How do you usually feel about ordinary weeks?

What might it look like to treat this one as meaningful rather than something to get through?

**Prayer**

Faithful God,
thank you for meeting me in the quiet weeks
when nothing feels urgent or new.
Help me trust that small acts of faith still matter
and that you are present in every ordinary day.
Amen.

# 25

# When You Do the Same Thing Again

"Let us not become weary in
doing good, for at the proper
time we will reap a harvest if we
do not give up." Galatians 6:9

There comes a point when faith feels repetitive.

Not difficult. Not dramatic. Just familiar.

You pray the same prayers. You cook the same meals. You show up to the same responsibilities. Nothing feels especially inspired, and nothing feels especially wrong. It's just the same thing again.

This is often where we grow restless.

We start to wonder whether repetition means stagnation. Whether doing the same thing again is a sign that we've stopped growing. Whether faith is supposed to feel more alive than this.

But repetition is not the enemy of faith.
It is one of its most faithful teachers.

At the counter, repetition looks like muscle memory.
You don't think about how to crack the eggs anymore.

You don't reread the recipe. Your hands know what to do. The work is quieter now, steadier, less anxious.

Faith works the same way.

There are seasons when growth is visible and energizing. And then there are seasons when faith is practiced simply by continuing. By doing what you know to do, even when it feels unremarkable.

Scripture reminds us not to grow weary in doing good, not because it will always feel rewarding, but because faithfulness has a longer horizon than our emotions.

Doing the same thing again can be an act of trust.

Trust that prayer still matters, even when it's brief.
Trust that care still counts, even when it's routine.
Trust that God is present, even when nothing feels especially holy.

Some weeks are not about learning something new. They are about staying with what has already been given. Letting faith settle into your bones. Allowing devotion to become habit, and habit to become home.

If this week feels repetitive, you're not doing it wrong.

You're practicing endurance.
You're learning how faith carries on.
You're showing up.

And that, too, is holy work.

**Soul Note**

Repetition is not failure. It is often the shape faith takes when it matures.

## Soul Pause

Where are you tempted to quit simply because something feels repetitive?

What might it look like to trust that faith is still forming you here?

## Prayer

Steady God,
when faith feels ordinary and repetitive,
help me trust the quiet work you are doing.
Give me patience for the long middle
and courage to keep showing up.
Amen.

# 26

# What Still Has Something to Give

"See, I am doing a new thing!
Now it springs up; do you not
perceive it?"
Isaiah 43:19

There are things we're tempted to throw away simply because they've been sitting too long.

Fruit that's past its prime. Plans that didn't unfold as expected. Parts of ourselves that feel worn, tired, or overused. We assume their usefulness has expired, and we move on without a second look.

But experience teaches us otherwise.

Some of the best things come from what looks overripe. From what has softened with time. From what no longer fits the original intention but still holds surprising sweetness.

In ordinary weeks, this truth matters.

When life is steady but unremarkable, we often overlook what's already in front of us. We wait for something fresh, something new, something that feels more promising. Meanwhile, God continues to work quietly with what we already have.

Faith in ordinary time is rarely about acquiring more. It's about noticing what still carries life.

There are seasons when we feel past our peak. When our energy has changed. When old dreams have shifted shape. It's easy to assume that usefulness belongs only to what is new and shiny and full of potential.

But God has never been limited by appearances.

Scripture is filled with stories of God bringing something unexpected out of what others dismissed. New life out of dry ground. Hope out of long waiting. Purpose out of places that seemed finished.

At the counter, this wisdom shows up in simple ways. You look at what's been sitting. You consider what could still be made. You resist the urge to discard too quickly.

The same patience applies to our lives.

You are not required to be at your freshest to be faithful.
You are not disqualified because something feels tired or familiar. Often, it is precisely what has endured that becomes the richest offering.

If you find yourself in an ordinary week, surrounded by things that feel used up or overlooked, pause before you clear them away. Ask what might still be possible here.

God is always doing a new thing.
Sometimes it just looks softer than we expected.

**Soul Note**

What feels past its prime may still be full of grace.

**Soul Pause**

What in your life are you tempted to dismiss because it feels worn or ordinary?

How might God be inviting you to see it differently?

**Prayer**

God of renewal,
help me trust that nothing you have shaped is wasted.
Teach me to notice what still has something to give
and to welcome new life in unexpected forms.
Amen.

# 27

# The Cake That Named Me

*The cake that started it all.*

"Do not forget to show
hospitality to strangers, for by
so doing some people have
shown hospitality to angels
without knowing it."
Hebrews 13:2

I didn't set out to earn a nickname.

It happened quietly, the way most meaningful things do.

One visit at a time. One kitchen table. One shared slice of cake and a cup of coffee.

While I was serving as a Synodically Appointed Minister, I made a habit of baking before home visits. Sometimes it was cake. Sometimes cinnamon rolls. Sometimes cookies. We would sit together, talk, pray, and share something sweet. And when it was time for me to leave, I would wrap up what was left and place it back in their kitchen.

The visit didn't end when I walked out the door. The care lingered.

Somewhere along the way, people started calling me *the Baking Pastor*.

At first, I laughed it off. But eventually, I realized what they were naming wasn't about baking at all. It was about the way food softened the room. The way sharing something homemade made space for conversation that mattered. The way hospitality opened hearts without forcing anything.

This banana cake was part of that story.

It's a crowd-pleaser in the truest sense. Familiar. Comforting. Not flashy. The kind of cake that feels appropriate whether someone is celebrating or grieving, whether the visit is joyful or heavy.

Hospitality doesn't require perfection. It doesn't require the right words. Often, it simply requires showing up with something to share and the willingness to stay awhile.

In ministry, I learned that faith often enters through ordinary doors. A kitchen counter. A dining table. A plate passed across the room. God's presence doesn't announce itself loudly. It arrives gently, wrapped in care.

This cake carries that truth.

It reminds me that my calling has always been rooted in presence. In sitting with people where they are. In trusting that God works through small acts of attention and kindness.

If you've ever wondered whether what you offer matters, let this be your reminder: hospitality is holy work. What you bring to the table can name you in ways you never expected.

# Crowd-Pleasing Banana Cake

*A recipe that helped earn the name "The Baking Pastor"*

## Cake Ingredients

- 2½ cups all-purpose flour

- 1 teaspoon salt

- ¾ teaspoon baking powder

- ¾ teaspoon baking soda

- 1⅔ cups sugar

- ⅔ cup shortening

- 2 eggs

- 1¼ cups mashed ripe bananas (2–3 medium)

- ⅔ cup buttermilk

- ⅔ cup sliced almonds, plus extra for garnish

## Frosting Ingredients

- ⅓ cup plus 2 tablespoons all-purpose flour

- Dash of salt

- 1 cup milk

- ½ cup shortening

- 1 stick butter, softened

- 1 1/4 cup granulated sugar

- 1 teaspoon almond extract

**Directions**

1. Preheat oven to 375°F. Grease and flour two 9-inch round cake pans.

2. In a medium bowl, combine flour, salt, baking powder, and baking soda. Set aside.

3. In a large bowl, beat sugar and shortening until light and fluffy. Add eggs one at a time, beating well after each addition. Blend in bananas.

4. Add flour mixture alternately with buttermilk, beating well after each addition. Stir in sliced almonds.

5. Pour batter evenly into prepared pans.

6. Bake 30–35 minutes, or until a toothpick inserted in the center comes out clean. Cool in pans 10 minutes, then remove to wire racks to cool completely.

7. Fill and frost with banana frosting. Garnish with banana slices and additional almonds if desired.

**Frosting Directions**

1. Combine flour and salt in a medium saucepan. Gradually stir in milk until well blended.

2. Cook over medium heat, stirring constantly, until thickened.

Let cool completely.

3. Beat shortening and butter together until creamy. Add sugar; beat until light and fluffy.

4. Beat in almond extract. Add cooled flour mixture and beat until smooth.

## Alternate Pan Option

You may also bake this cake in a 13 × 9-inch pan. Bake at 350°F for 30–35 minutes. Cool, frost, and garnish as desired.

## Soul Note

Hospitality doesn't have to be elaborate to be faithful. What you offer with care often speaks louder than words.

## Soul Pause

How have small acts of hospitality shaped your relationships or calling?

What do you already have that could be shared in love?

## Prayer

God of welcome and presence,
thank you for the ways you meet us through shared tables
and ordinary acts of care.
Help me trust that what I offer, given in love,
is enough.
Amen.

# 28

# When You're the One Who Needs to Be Fed

"Martha, Martha," the Lord
answered, "you are worried
and upset about many things,
but few things are needed—or
indeed only one."
Luke 10:41–42

If you're someone who feeds others, receiving
care can feel uncomfortable.

You know how to bring the cake. You know how to set the table. You know how to read a room and notice what's needed before anyone asks. Hospitality has become second nature, woven into who you are and how you love.

Which makes it surprisingly hard to sit down when someone else offers.

I've learned that there are seasons when the most faithful thing you can do is let yourself be fed. Not because you've failed at caring, but because you're human. Because giving endlessly without receiving eventually empties the well.

Scripture gives us this quiet tension in the story of Martha and Mary. Martha is busy tending the work of hospitality, doing what she knows to do. Mary chooses to sit, to receive, to be present without producing anything. Jesus doesn't scold Martha for serving, but he gently reminds her that receiving is not a lesser calling.

Being fed is not passive.
It is an act of trust.

Trust that others are capable of care.
Trust that you are worthy of attention.
Trust that God's grace is not dependent on your output.

In the kitchen, this can be as simple as letting someone else cook the meal. Accepting the container of leftovers without insisting you didn't need it. Sitting down while someone else pours the coffee.

In faith, it looks like allowing prayer to be spoken over you instead of always offering it. Letting silence hold you without filling it. Receiving kindness without rushing to repay it.

If you're in a season where your energy is limited, or your spirit is tired, hear this gently: you are still faithful when you receive. You are still generous when you allow others to give. Love does not flow in only one direction.

Sometimes the table is set for you.

And choosing to sit down is not selfish.
It is honest.
It is holy.

**Soul Note**

Receiving care is not weakness. It is part of how God sustains us.

**Soul Pause**

Where do you resist being cared for, even when it's offered freely?

What might change if you allowed yourself to receive without explanation?

**Prayer**

God of abundance and mercy,
teach me to receive with the same grace
with which I try to give.
Help me trust that your care comes through others
and that I do not have to earn rest.
Amen.

# 29

# When You Need to Feed a Lot of People

"How can I set this before
a hundred men?" his servant
asked. But Elisha answered,
"Give it to the people to eat.
For this is what the Lord says:
'They will eat and have some
left over.'" 2 Kings 4:43

There comes a moment when care has to scale.

Not because you're trying to be impressive, but because the need is bigger than one person, one visit, one carefully planned offering. The room fills. The list grows. The situation shifts from *personal* to *communal*.

And suddenly, the question becomes simple and urgent: *How do we feed everyone?*

This is not the moment for complexity.

When many people need nourishment, faith doesn't ask for perfection. It asks for wisdom. For food that stretches. For something warm and filling and forgiving. For a meal that can be ladled without ceremony and received without explanation.

Scripture understands this moment well. Again and again, God meets abundance with simplicity. Not extravagance, but sufficiency. Not fuss, but trust. The miracle is rarely in what's offered. It's in the willingness to place it on the table.

In ordinary life, this kind of care shows up in casseroles, soup pots, and meals that can be doubled without stress. Food that doesn't mind waiting. Food that tastes better the next day. Food that welcomes people as they are.

This is where hospitality becomes practical.

Feeding many people doesn't require you to know everyone's story. It doesn't require the right words. It requires a pot big enough to hold what's needed and the courage to believe it will be enough.

There is a quiet humility in meals like this. They don't draw attention to themselves. They serve the moment. They make room for conversation, for grief, for laughter, for silence.

And they remind us that God often works through what we already know how to do.

If you're facing a moment when the need feels larger than your capacity, take heart. You don't have to feed everyone perfectly. You just have to feed them faithfully.

Sometimes that means putting something simple on the stove and trusting that God will do the rest.

**Soul Note**

When care is shared widely, simplicity becomes an act of wisdom.

## Soul Pause

Where are you feeling asked to care for more than feels manageable?

What simple offering might be enough for this moment?

## Prayer

God of provision,
when the need feels larger than my strength,
help me trust the gifts already in my hands
.Teach me to offer what I have
and believe that you will make it enough.
Amen.

# 30

# The Chili That Holds Us Together

"Invest in seven ventures, yes,
in eight, for you do not know
what disaster may come upon
the land." Ecclesiastes 11:2

Chili is a meal that understands flexibility.

It doesn't insist on one right way. It welcomes variations. It stretches when more people arrive and forgives substitutions when the pantry looks thin. It's the kind of food that shows up when life is unpredictable and still manages to feel grounding.

That's part of its gift.

When care needs to reach many people, chili meets the moment. It feeds bodies without demanding attention. It allows conversation to flow. It can sit on the stove while stories unfold and still be good when everyone finally comes back for seconds.

Chili holds space.

In our house, chili also holds a friendly debate. Beans or no beans. Turkey or beef. Thicker or thinner. Spicier or mild. These differences don't divide us. They remind us that nourishment doesn't have to be uniform to be faithful.

In community, this matters.

There are seasons when people arrive at the table with different needs, different tolerances, different preferences. Hospitality doesn't flatten those differences. It makes room for them. It says, *there's space here for how you show up*.

Chili teaches us that care can be practical and generous at the same time. That feeding many doesn't require perfection. That warmth and sustenance often matter more than agreement.

If you're tending a moment that feels communal, uncertain, or stretched, consider what kind of care will hold people together rather than impress them. Choose what can adapt. Choose what welcomes conversation. Choose what lasts.

Sometimes faith looks like a big pot on the stove and the trust that it will be enough.

## Laura's Chili Recipe
## (With Beans)

**Ingredients**

- 1 lb. ground turkey or chicken *(beef may also be used)*

- 2 cans (8 oz) tomato sauce

- 2 cans (15 oz) kidney beans, drained and rinsed

- 1 can (8 oz) chicken broth

- 1 ½ tablespoons chili powder

- 1 tablespoon cumin

- 1 teaspoon garlic powder

- 1 teaspoon onion powder

- 1 teaspoon paprika

- 1 teaspoon oregano

- ½ teaspoon cayenne pepper (adjust for heat)

- Salt and pepper to taste

- Masa flour (optional, for thickening)

**Optional Toppings:**

Shredded cheese, sour cream, avocado

**Directions**

1. Brown the ground turkey or chicken in a large skillet; drain excess fat.

2. Add tomato sauce, beans, broth, and spices. Stir well to combine.

3. Simmer covered for about 30 minutes, stirring occasionally. Adjust heat with cayenne pepper if desired.

4. For thicker chili, mix 1–2 tablespoons Masa flour with water to form a paste. Stir into chili and simmer an additional 5 minutes.

**Serving Suggestions:**

Serve with cornbread or tortilla chips. Top as desired.

**In our house, this care takes more than one form.**

# Todd's Chili
# (No Beans)

*A classic, straightforward chili that keeps things simple and familiar.*

## Ingredients

- 1 lb. ground meat *(Todd uses beef, but any ground meat works)*

- 1 cup water

- 1 small onion, grated *(reserve the juice)*

- 1 teaspoon salt

- 1 teaspoon black pepper

## Add after browning:

- ½ teaspoon white sugar

- 1 tablespoon chili powder

- 1 cup ketchup

- 1 teaspoon mustard

- Dash of Worcestershire sauce

## Directions

1. In a large skillet or pot, brown the ground meat over medium heat. Drain excess fat if needed.

2. Add water, grated onion (including the juice), salt, and pepper. Stir to combine.

3. Add sugar, chili powder, ketchup, mustard, and Worcestershire sauce. Mix well.

4. Cover and let simmer gently for 1 hour, stirring occasionally.

5. Taste and adjust seasoning as desired.

## Serving Notes

This chili is simple, comforting, and unfussy. It's especially good served:

- on hotdogs

- with crackers or cornbread

## Soul Note

Hospitality doesn't require agreement. It requires care that adapts.

## Soul Pause

Where might flexibility serve love better than certainty right now?

How can you offer nourishment without insisting on one right way?

**Prayer**

God of abundance and grace,
teach me to offer care that holds people together.
Help me make room for difference,
and trust that what is shared in love is enough.
Amen.

# 31

# After Everyone Has Eaten

"Then, because so many
people were coming and going
that they did not even have a
chance to eat, he said to them,
'Come with me by yourselves
to a quiet place and get some
rest.'" Mark 6:31

There's a particular quiet that comes after hospitality.

The pot is empty or cooling on the stove. Chairs are pushed back under the table. The sink is full, but it can wait. The house exhales in a way it couldn't while everyone was still here.

This is a holy moment, even if it doesn't feel dramatic.

After feeding others, it's tempting to rush straight into cleanup or planning the next thing. We're good at staying busy. We're less practiced at stopping long enough to notice what just happened. But faith invites us to pause, to let the moment land.

Jesus knew this rhythm well. Again and again, he gathered people, fed them, healed them, taught them. And then he withdrew. Not because the work wasn't important, but because rest was part of the work itself.

Care has an aftermath.

There is joy in having fed people, and there is also tiredness. Both are honest. Ignoring either one makes the work harder than it needs to be. When we skip the pause, we miss the chance to receive what the moment offered us in return.

In the kitchen, this pause might look like sitting down at the counter for a minute before washing the dishes. Letting the quiet stretch just a little. Noticing the way the house feels when it's empty again.

In faith, it looks like allowing rest to follow generosity. Letting silence come without filling it. Trusting that you don't have to prove anything now.

This is not laziness.
It is wisdom.

The work of hospitality doesn't end when everyone leaves. It completes itself in rest. In reflection. In the gentle acknowledgment that something meaningful just took place.

If you've recently poured yourself out, give yourself permission to stop for a moment. The dishes will still be there. The next need will come soon enough. For now, let the quiet hold you.

God meets us not only in the giving, but in the resting afterward.

**Soul Note**

Rest after care is not indulgence. It is part of faithful living.

## Soul Pause

What helps you transition from giving to resting?

Where might God be inviting you to pause instead of pushing on?

## Prayer

God who sees and sustains,
thank you for the work of caring and the gift of rest.
Help me honor both, and trust that you are present
even in the quiet after the work is done.
Amen.

# 32

# Something Cool After the Heat

"Like cold water to a weary
soul is good news from a
distant land." Proverbs 25:25

After the pot has simmered and the house has finally gone quiet,
something cool feels like mercy.

This is the moment after the work is done. After the conversations
have wound down. After the dishes are stacked and the counter has
been wiped clean. It's the point where your body realizes it can rest,
and your spirit follows.

Not everything restorative is heavy.

Sometimes care comes cold from the refrigerator.
Something light.
Something that doesn't demand attention or explanation.
Something that simply refreshes.

Old-fashioned icebox desserts were made for moments like this. They
don't rely on heat or hurry. They wait patiently, becoming what they
need to be over time. Their goodness comes not from effort, but from
restraint.

This kind of care matters.

In faith, we often focus on endurance. On holding steady through difficulty. On staying present when things are hard. But Scripture also speaks of refreshment. Of relief. Of goodness that meets us when we're tired and says, *You can stop now.*

Cooling down after intensity is part of faithful living.

The icebox pie reminds me that not every offering has to be warm and filling. Some are meant to soothe. To reset. To lighten the body and spirit after long stretches of effort.

If you've just come through something demanding, let yourself receive what refreshes you. Not everything that heals feels profound. Sometimes it feels like a cool slice on a warm day, shared slowly, without expectation.

God's care arrives in many forms.

Sometimes it arrives chilled and waiting.

# Old-Fashioned Lemon Icebox Pie

*A cool, refreshing dessert for after the work is done.*

## Ingredients

- 1 (7-ounce) package Goya Maria cookies(*If you can't find Maria cookies, you can use 12 graham cracker sheets*)

- ½ cup butter, melted

- 2 (8-ounce) packages cream cheese, softened

- 1 (14-ounce) can sweetened condensed milk

- Juice of 2 lemons

- 1 teaspoon lemon zest

- Whipped cream, for garnish

- Mint leaves (optional)

**Directions**

1. Preheat oven to 325°F.

2. In a food processor, pulse cookies until fine crumbs form. Add melted butter and pulse until combined.

3. Press mixture evenly into the bottom (and sides, if desired) of a pie pan to about ¼-inch thickness.

4. Bake for 8–10 minutes, until golden, crisp, and firm. Let cool completely.

5. In a medium bowl, beat cream cheese until fluffy.

6. Add sweetened condensed milk, lemon juice, and lemon zest. Mix until smooth.

7. Pour lemon mixture into cooled crust.

8. Refrigerate for at least 2 hours before serving.

9. Garnish with whipped cream and mint leaves if desired. Slice and serve.

**Soul Note**

Restoration does not always arrive through effort. Sometimes it comes through refreshment.

**Soul Pause**

What helps you cool down after seasons of intensity?

Where might God be offering relief rather than more responsibility?

**Prayer**

God of gentle mercy,
thank you for moments of refreshment
that meet us when we are weary.
Help me receive rest without guilt
and trust that relief is part of your care.
Amen.

# 33

# When Good Things Take Time

"In vain you rise early and
stay up late, toiling for food
to eat— for he grants sleep to
those he loves." Psalm 127:2

Some goodness cannot be hurried.

There are foods that ask you to slow down. To wait. To trust the process instead of forcing an outcome. They don't respond well to shortcuts, and they're not impressed by efficiency. What they offer in return is worth the patience they require.

This is true in the kitchen, and it is true in faith.

We live in a culture that praises speed. Faster answers. Quicker fixes. Immediate results. Waiting can feel like weakness, like wasted time, like something to push through rather than honor.

But some things are only made well by waiting.

In ordinary life, this shows up in mornings that unfold slowly. When the house is quiet. When the day hasn't yet demanded anything from you. When you can take your time without feeling behind.

These moments teach us something about trust.

God's work often unfolds at a pace that resists our urgency. Growth happens beneath the surface. Healing takes its own time. Joy deepens gradually, not all at once. Trying to rush these processes usually leaves us with something unfinished.

Slow goodness reminds us that patience is not passive. It is attentive. It stays present while something becomes what it's meant to be.

In faith, waiting can feel uncomfortable. We'd rather act, fix, decide, move on. But waiting, when chosen rather than endured, becomes a form of worship. It says, *I trust that God is at work even when I am not pushing.*

If your life feels slower than you expected right now, resist the urge to label it as wasted time. Ask instead what might be forming quietly. What goodness is taking shape while you wait.

Some of the most meaningful moments arrive not because we rushed toward them, but because we allowed ourselves to linger.

Good things take time.

And time, when received rather than resisted, becomes a gift.

**Soul Note**

Waiting does not mean nothing is happening. Often, it means something is being made ready.

**Soul Pause**

Where are you tempted to rush what needs time?

What might change if you allowed patience to be part of your faith this
week?

**Prayer**

God of steady work,
help me trust your timing
even when I wish things would move faster.
Teach me to wait with hope
and receive the good you are forming slowly.
Amen.

# 34

# What We Keep Alive

"One generation commends
your works to another; they tell
of your mighty acts."
Psalm 145:4

Some things are not made once.

They are kept.

Sourdough starter is like that. It isn't impressive at first glance. It looks ordinary. A little messy. Easy to forget in the back of the refrigerator if you aren't paying attention. But it's alive. And it only stays alive if someone remembers to tend it.

The starter recipe came from my grandmother, Nannie. It has been fed, rested, stirred, and shared across years and kitchens. It has traveled through hands that knew how to wait. Hands that understood that good things don't need to be rushed to be real.

When I bake cinnamon rolls with it, I'm not just following a recipe. I'm participating in something that was already in motion long before I arrived.

Faith works like that too.

We often talk about belief as something we decide or achieve. But more often, it's something we inherit. Something we're handed, sometimes quietly, by people who lived it in front of us. Faith is kept alive through ordinary acts of care. Through showing up. Through repetition. Through patience.

This dough doesn't hurry. It rests. It stretches. It folds back into itself. It waits again. Time does the work that force never could.

There are seasons when faith feels like that. When nothing dramatic is happening. When growth is slow and invisible. When all you can do is tend what you've been given and trust that it's enough.

This is not wasted time.

Keeping something alive is holy work.

Every time I make these rolls, I think about what has been passed to me. Not just a starter, but a way of being. A trust that goodness grows quietly. A belief that care given over time multiplies.

If your faith feels small right now, don't discard it. Feed it. Let it rest. Give it time. What's alive doesn't need to prove itself. It just needs to be tended.

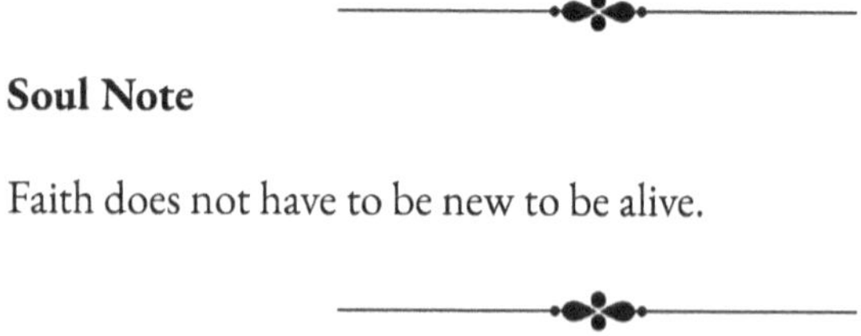

**Soul Note**

Faith does not have to be new to be alive.

**Soul Pause**

What practices, people, or stories have kept your faith alive over time?

What might it look like to tend them again?

## Prayer

God of generations,
thank you for the faith that was handed to me
before I knew how to name it.
Help me tend what you've entrusted to me
with patience, care, and hope.
Amen.

**Kitchen Note:** Nannie's starter is gluten-free (made with potato flakes). Recipes may be adapted with a 1-to-1 gluten-free flour blend.

# Cinnamon Rolls
# with Nannie's Sourdough Starter

*A slow, generous recipe meant to be shared.*

## Ingredients

## Dough

- 1 cup fed sourdough starter

- ¾ cup milk, lukewarm

- 1 large egg

- 4 tablespoons butter, softened

- 4¾–6 cups (594–750 g) all-purpose flour (depending on starter thickness)

- ½ cup (57 g) wheat flour

- ¼ cup granulated sugar

- 1½ teaspoons table salt

- 1 teaspoon instant yeast, optional*

**Filling**

- ¾ cup light or dark brown sugar, packed

- ¼ cup (30 g) unbleached all-purpose flour

- 1 tablespoon cinnamon

- ⅛ teaspoon table salt

- ¼ cup butter, melted

**Icing**

- 1½ cups confectioners' sugar

- Pinch of salt (optional)

- 1½ tablespoons butter

- 1 tablespoon pure vanilla extract

- ¼ cup heavy cream

**Instructions**

**To make the dough:**

Weigh your flour, or measure by gently spooning into a cup and leveling. Mix all dough ingredients *except* salt (and yeast) until evenly moistened and sticky, about 2–3 minutes on low speed. (A Danish whisk works well.)

Add salt (and yeast, if using) on top of the dough without mixing. Cover and rest 20 minutes. Mix to incorporate, about 1 minute. Knead until smooth and supple but still soft and tacky, 2–3 minutes.

Cover and rest in a warm place (about 75°F) for 4 hours. Stretch and fold the dough 3–4 times during this rest, roughly once per hour.

**To make the filling:**

Combine all filling ingredients in a medium bowl until thick.

Turn dough onto a lightly greased or floured surface. Gently deflate and roll into a 14″ × 20″ rectangle. Spread filling evenly, leaving ½″ bare along one short edge. Roll tightly from the filled edge into a log, about 18″ long.

Cut into twelve 1½″ slices and place in a lightly greased 9″ × 13″ pan. Cover and let rise until puffy, 2–3 hours.

At this point, either:

- Bake the same day, or

- Refrigerate overnight (up to 24 hours), covered, and bake the next day.

**To bake same day:**

Bake at 400°F for 18–22 minutes, until golden and center reaches 190°F.

**To bake after refrigeration:**

Let rolls rest at room temperature while oven preheats to 400°F. Bake 20–25 minutes, until golden and center reaches 190°F.

**To make the icing:**

Stir all icing ingredients until smooth. Ice rolls after cooling 5–10 minutes.

Store covered at room temperature for one day or freeze unfrosted rolls for longer storage.

** Optional yeast shortens rise times if starter isn't fully ripe.*

# Section V: Trusting the Story That Holds Us

Learning to live from nearness rather than certainty.

# 35

# When Your Thoughts Won't Slow Down

"Do not be anxious about
anything, but in every
situation, by prayer and
petition, with thanksgiving,
present your requests to God."
Philippians 4:6

There are moments when your mind refuses to clock out.

Thoughts pile up like dishes left too long in the sink. One worry leans into the next. Questions echo. What-ifs tap insistently at the edges of the night.

You try to quiet them.
You tell yourself to calm down.
You promise you'll deal with it tomorrow.

But your thoughts keep stirring.

An anxious mind can feel like dough that's been worked too much. The more you handle it, the tighter everything becomes. Peace feels just out of reach, not because you're doing something wrong, but because you're doing too much.

Sometimes the most faithful move is to set the bowl down.

God is not alarmed by your racing thoughts.
God is not waiting for you to fix them before drawing near.

You don't need perfect calm to be held.
You don't need silence to be faithful.

You are allowed to bring the noise with you.

**Soul Note**

Rest doesn't always mean your thoughts stop. Sometimes it means you stop arguing with them.

**Soul Pause**

Take a slow breath .Unclench your jaw. Let your shoulders drop.

Imagine setting your thoughts on the counter like a pile of ingredients.
You don't have to combine them.
You don't have to clean them up.
Just let them be seen and held.

**Prayer**

God of steady presence,
when my thoughts won't slow down,
hold what I cannot quiet.
Give me rest that doesn't depend on answers.
Amen.

# 36

# You Don't Have to Carry Tomorrow Today

"Therefore do not worry
about tomorrow, for
tomorrow will worry about
itself. Each day has enough
trouble of its own."
Matthew 6:34

There's a quiet weight that shows up when tomorrow starts leaning into today.

Plans. Appointments. Conversations you haven't had yet. Outcomes you're already rehearsing in your head.

Tomorrow has a way of sneaking onto the counter before you're ready.

You tell yourself you're just being prepared. Responsible. Thoughtful. But what you're really doing is carrying more than this moment requires. And it's exhausting.

In the kitchen, there's a difference between gathering ingredients and trying to bake everything at once. Some things belong on the counter now. Others stay on the shelf until their time comes.

Your soul works the same way.

You are not meant to live several days at the same time.
You are not required to solve future problems with today's limited strength. Grace arrives in daily portions, not bulk storage.

What's needed for this moment will be given for this moment.

Tomorrow will have its own counter space. Its own breath. Its own grace.

For now, today is enough.

## Soul Note

Carrying tomorrow early doesn't make you more faithful.

It only makes today heavier than it needs to be.

## Soul Pause

What future moment are you already carrying today?

What would it look like to set that down, just for now?

What is actually being asked of you in this moment, not the next one?

## Prayer

God of daily grace,
teach me to live where my feet are.
Help me trust that tomorrow will be met
with the strength You provide when it arrives.
Amen.

# 37

# Waiting Is Still a Way of Showing Up

"Wait for the Lord; be strong
and take heart and wait for the
Lord." Psalm 27:14

Waiting has a bad reputation.

It feels passive. Unproductive. Like time slipping through your fingers while nothing happens.

We prefer movement. Progress. Clear steps and visible results. Waiting feels like standing still while the world keeps spinning.

But in the kitchen, waiting is never wasted.

Dough rises while you step away. Flavors deepen while the pot simmers. Heat does its quiet work long before anything looks finished. What appears still is often doing more than you realize.

Waiting is not absence.
It is presence without control.

So much of life requires this kind of showing up. Sitting with uncertainty. Staying when you'd rather rush ahead.

Trusting that something is forming beneath the surface, even when you can't see it yet.

You are not behind because you're waiting.
You are not failing because the next step hasn't appeared.

Sometimes faith looks like staying put and letting time and grace do their work.

**Soul Note**

Waiting doesn't mean nothing is happening.

It means something is happening quietly.

**Soul Pause**

Where in your life are you being asked to wait right now?

What would it look like to stay present instead of forcing movement?

Can you trust that growth is happening even if you can't see it yet?

**Prayer**

God of unseen work,
help me wait without fear.
Give me patience when I want control
and trust when I want certainty.
Amen.

# 38

# You Are Allowed to Be Here

> "In repentance and rest is
> your salvation, in quietness
> and trust is your strength..."
> Isaiah 30:15

There are days when simply being present feels like an accomplishment.

No progress to report. No clarity gained. Just you, showing up as you are.

That is enough.

We live with the quiet pressure to justify our place. To prove we're growing. Healing. Doing something useful with our time and pain. But not every moment asks for movement.

Some moments ask for presence.

At the counter, there are times when nothing is being prepared. The space is cleared. The bowl is empty. The kitchen is still. And yet, the room is not wasted.

You are not wasting space when you pause.
You are not behind because nothing looks finished.

You are allowed to be here.
Right now. As you are.

••••

**Soul Note**

Presence does not need permission.

••••

**Soul Pause**

What would it look like to stop explaining yourself today?

Where can you let your worth be assumed instead of earned?

What happens if you allow this moment to be enough?

••••

**Prayer**

God of gentle nearness,
help me rest in being held.
Teach me that presence is not a pause from faith,
but one of its deepest expressions.
Amen.

# 39

# Something Warm to Keep on Hand

"That each of them may eat
and drink, and find satisfaction
in all their toil—this is the gift
of God." Ecclesiastes 3:13

Some days don't need fixing.

They need warming.

Cold, dreary days have a way of settling into your bones. Not dramatic enough to demand attention. Not urgent enough to rearrange your plans. Just heavy enough to make everything feel slower.

Those are the days when it helps to have something ready.

I learned this years ago at a holiday craft show, walking the aisles with my mom and my grandparents, Gam and Popi. Among the quilts and ornaments sat a small jar of Old-Fashioned Russian Tea mix. Nothing fancy. Just promise in a jar.

Mom and I loved it. One cup, several teaspoons of mix stirred into hot water, and suddenly the day softened. It became a small ritual. A quiet comfort. Something we reached for when the world felt gray.

I eventually tracked down the recipe so I could keep a big batch on hand. Not for special occasions. For ordinary ones. The kind of days that don't announce their need but feel better once you're holding a warm mug.

The soul needs that kind of preparation too.

You won't always know when a hard day is coming. But you can keep small comforts nearby. Familiar prayers. Gentle routines. Recipes that remind you that cheer can be mixed up when you need it.

You don't have to wait for joy to appear out of nowhere. Sometimes you make a cup.

**Soul Note**

Preparation isn't about control.

It's about care.

**Soul Pause**

What small comfort do you keep within reach for hard or heavy days?

Is there something simple you could prepare now for a future moment of need?

Who taught you how to offer warmth, and how might you pass that on?

**Prayer**

God of simple comforts,
thank You for warmth that can be held
and care that can be prepared ahead of time.
Teach me to tend my soul
with the same gentleness I offer others.
Amen.

# Old-Fashioned Russian Tea Mix

*A cup of cheer to keep on hand*

This is the kind of recipe you don't make for a single afternoon.

You make it so it's there when you need it.

Mixed once, stored simply, and ready whenever a cold, dreary day settles in, this tea has a way of softening the edges. It's bright and spiced and comforting all at once. A reminder that warmth can be prepared ahead of time.

**Ingredients**

- 1 cup instant tea mix, unsweetened

- 1 ¾ cups instant lemonade mix

- 20 ounces Tang

- 1 ½ teaspoons ground cinnamon

- 1 ½ teaspoons ground cloves

**Instructions**

1. Place all ingredients into a large zip-top bag.

2. Seal and shake until the mixture is evenly blended.

3. Pour into clean glass jars and seal tightly.

**To Serve**

Add 2–3 teaspoons of tea mix to a mug of boiling water, adjusting to taste. Leave a little room at the top of the mug. This tea likes to fizz before it settles.

**At the Counter Notes**

- This recipe makes a generous batch, perfect for keeping on hand through the season.

- It also makes a thoughtful gift. Poured into jars and sealed tight, it carries warmth far beyond your own kitchen.

- When someone drinks it, they may not know your whole story, but they'll feel the care behind it.

Sometimes comfort isn't complicated.

Sometimes it's already mixed, waiting quietly on the shelf.

Mix up a batch.
Print a few tags.
Tie them on with twine.
Share warmth when it's needed most.

**Suggested Uses**

- Gift jars at holidays

- Care packages

- Church events

- Soul Care Circle gatherings

- A quiet "thinking of you" moment

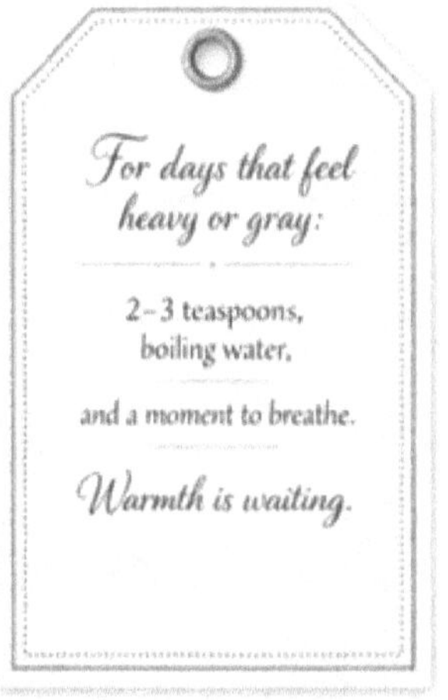

# 40

# Care Has a Way of Multiplying

"They broke bread in their
homes and ate together
with glad and sincere hearts,
praising God." Acts 2:46

Warmth rarely stays where it starts.

You make a cup for yourself, and suddenly you're thinking of someone else. Someone who might be tired. Someone who's been quiet lately. Someone who could use a small kindness without having to ask for it.

Care does that.
It moves.

At the counter, you often start with one portion and end up sharing more than you planned. An extra cookie wrapped up. A jar filled twice. A tag tied on because it felt right.

Not because you were obligated.
Because generosity has momentum.

You don't have to be overflowing to offer something meaningful. You don't need abundance to practice care. You only need awareness. A willingness to notice where warmth might be needed next.

Sometimes the most faithful thing you do is pass along what steadied you. No explanation required. No lesson attached. Just a quiet offering that says, "I thought of you."

Care multiplies when it's shared freely, not strategically.

---

**Soul Note**

You don't have to give everything away to give something meaningful.

---

**Soul Pause**

Who comes to mind when you think about sharing warmth?

What small gesture could feel natural, not forced?

Where might care already be moving through you?

---

**Prayer**

God of generous love,
help me notice where care wants to go next.
Teach me to share gently,
without pressure or performance.
Amen.

# 41

# When Care Comes Back to You

"Carry each other's burdens,
and in this way you will fulfill
the law of Christ."
Galatians 6:2

Receiving care can feel surprisingly vulnerable.

You know how to give it. You're practiced at noticing needs, anticipating gaps, offering warmth before anyone asks. That part feels familiar. Safe, even.

But when care turns toward you, something in you stiffens. I learned this the hard way during chemotherapy. I was not good at asking for help. I wanted to manage. To stay independent. To prove I could still hold everything together.

But chemo has a way of humbling you.

There were days I hadn't slept. Days my body felt heavy and uncooperative. Days when I had just laid down, finally, when Todd's phone rang. Someone was on the way with a meal.

Everything in me wanted to say no. It would have been easier. More efficient. Kinder, I told myself.

But I learned something in that season. When I refused, I wasn't just protecting my tired body. I was denying someone else the chance to love freely.

So I got up. I waited. I received the hospitality.

Not because I felt strong.
But because love was being offered.

At the counter, it's often easier to keep working than to sit down and let someone else take over. Easier to keep serving than to accept the plate handed back to you.

But care is not meant to move in only one direction.

Receiving is not weakness.
It is trust.

It says, "I believe this is being offered without strings.
"It says, "I don't have to earn what's freely given."

Letting care come back to you doesn't undo your strength. It reminds you that you don't stand alone at the counter.

**Soul Note**

Receiving care is not failing at self-sufficiency.

It is practicing belonging.

**Soul Pause**

What makes it hard for you to receive help or kindness?

Who has offered care that you may have quietly pushed away?

What would it look like to say yes, even when it feels inconvenient?

**Prayer**

God of shared tables,
help me receive what is offered in love.
Loosen my need to prove my worth,
and teach me to rest in belonging.
Amen.

# 42

# You Don't Owe Anyone for Being Loved

"For it is by grace you have been
saved, through faith— and this
is not from yourselves, it is the
gift of God— not by works,
so that no one can boast."
Ephesians 2:8–9

After care is received, something else often follows.

A quiet discomfort. A mental ledger.

You start counting.
How will I repay this?
When can I make it even?
What do I owe now?

Gratitude quietly turns into pressure. But love is not a transaction. At the counter, hospitality is offered freely or it isn't hospitality at all. You don't tally who brought what. You don't measure worth by contribution. You trust that what's shared is enough.

Care works the same way.

When someone shows up for you, they are not asking for repayment. They are responding to love already moving in them. Your job is not to balance the books. It's to receive with honesty and let gratitude stay light.

You honor care not by returning it immediately, but by letting it shape you.

By resting.
By healing.
By remembering how it felt to be held.

The time for sharing will come again. It always does.
But it doesn't have to be rushed.

**Soul Note**

Gratitude doesn't require repayment.

It requires presence.

**Soul Pause**

Where have you felt pressure to "make up for" care you received?

What would it look like to let gratitude exist without obligation?

Can you trust that love offered freely is complete as it is?

## Prayer

God of unearned grace,
help me receive love without keeping score.
Teach me gratitude that rests,
and generosity that flows in its own time.
Amen.

# 43

# The Quiet Strength of Ordinary Days

"Whatever you do, work at it
with all your heart, as working
for the Lord..."
Colossians 3:23

Resilience often gets dressed up as bravery.

Big moments. Hard conversations. Turning points, we can point to later and say, "That's when I made it through."

But most resilience is quieter than that.

It looks like getting up again. Making the bed. Drinking water. Returning to the counter even when nothing feels inspiring. Choosing steadiness over intensity.

At the counter, resilience isn't about elaborate meals or perfect timing. It's about showing up for the basics. Feeding yourself. Cleaning one small space. Trusting that simple care counts.

Ordinary days don't announce their importance. They just keep coming.

And you keep meeting them.

That is not weakness.
That is strength that lasts.

You don't need to be impressive to be resilient. You need to be faithful to what's in front of you. Again. And again.

This kind of resilience doesn't burn bright and fast.
It warms slowly.
It sustains.

**Soul Note**

Strength doesn't always roar.

Sometimes it whispers, "I'm still here."

**Soul Pause**

What ordinary practices help you keep going?

Where have you underestimated the strength it takes to tend daily life?

What would it look like to honor your consistency instead of dismissing it?

**Prayer**

God of daily mercies,
thank You for strength that meets me in ordinary moments.
Help me trust that showing up again is more than enough.
Amen.

# 44

# Starting Over Still Counts

"Forget the former things; do
not dwell on the past. See, I am
doing a new thing!"
Isaiah 43:18–19

Starting over doesn't always look like a fresh page.

Sometimes it looks like yesterday, again. The same kitchen. The same questions. The same weariness you hoped would be gone by now.

We tend to imagine starting over as a clean break. A clear line between before and after. But most of the time, it's quieter than that. You wake up. You try again. You do the next small thing.

At the counter, starting over often begins with crumbs. A surface that needs wiping. A bowl that gets washed so it can be used again. Nothing dramatic. Just readiness.

You don't have to feel hopeful to begin again.
You don't need energy or confidence or a plan.

You only need willingness.

Starting over still counts, even when it feels ordinary. Even when it happens more than once. Even when no one notices but you.

Every small beginning is a form of courage.

---

## Soul Note

Starting over doesn't erase the past.

It honors the choice to keep going.

---

## Soul Pause

Where are you being invited to begin again, even quietly?

What small step could mark a fresh start today?

What would it look like to release the pressure to make it feel new?

---

## Prayer

God of fresh mercies,
meet me in the act of beginning again.
Bless my willingness, however small,
and carry me forward one step at a time.
Amen.

# Easy Blueberry Muffins with Crumb Topping

*For mornings when you're beginning again*

Starting over doesn't need ceremony. Sometimes it begins with preheating the oven and trusting that something good can come from simple ingredients.

These muffins are soft, forgiving, and generous. They don't require perfection. They just ask you to begin.

## Ingredients

### Muffins

- 2 cups all-purpose flour *(set aside a few tablespoons to coat the blueberries)*

- ¾ cup granulated sugar

- 1 tablespoon baking powder

- ½ teaspoon salt

- 1 cup milk

- 2 large eggs

- ¼ cup butter, melted

- 1 teaspoon vanilla extract

- 1 cup blueberries, fresh or frozen *(do not thaw if using frozen)*

**Crumb Topping**

- ½ cup granulated sugar

- ⅓ cup all-purpose flour

- ¼ cup butter, cubed

- 1½ teaspoons ground cinnamon

**Instructions**

1. Preheat the oven to 400°F. Grease a 12-cup muffin pan or line with paper liners.

2. In a large bowl, whisk together the flour, sugar, baking powder, and salt.

3. In a separate bowl, whisk the milk, eggs, melted butter, and vanilla.

4. Add the wet ingredients to the dry ingredients and mix just until combined. Do not overmix.

5. Toss the blueberries with the reserved flour, then gently fold them into the batter.

6. To make the crumb topping, combine sugar, flour, butter, and cinnamon in a small bowl. Use a fork to mix until crumbly.

7. Spoon batter into the prepared muffin cups, filling each about three-quarters full. Sprinkle generously with crumb topping.

8. Bake for 20–22 minutes, or until a toothpick inserted in the center comes out clean. Allow muffins to cool slightly before

serving.

**At the Counter Tips**

- Coating the blueberries with flour keeps them evenly distributed throughout the muffins. Every bite matters.

- Fresh blueberries help keep the batter from turning blue or purple, but frozen work beautifully too.

- Mix gently. Overworking the batter makes muffins dense. Starting over doesn't require force.

- Store at room temperature for 3–5 days, or freeze for up to 3–4 months for future mornings.

Sometimes starting over looks like wiping the counter.
Sometimes it looks like muffins cooling on the rack.
Both count.

# 45

# The Small Joys That Carry You

"Every good and perfect gift
is from above, coming down
from the Father of the heavenly
lights, who does not change
like shifting shadows."
James 1:17

Joy doesn't always arrive loudly.

Sometimes it slips in quietly. A warm muffin. A clean mug. A moment when your shoulders drop and you realize you're breathing more easily than you were a minute ago.

We often wait for joy to feel complete or overwhelming. Something big enough to outweigh what's been hard. But joy that lasts tends to be smaller than that.

It shows up in ordinary kindness. Familiar routines. Comfort you didn't know you needed until it arrived.

At the counter, joy is rarely extravagant. It's the smell of something baking. The satisfaction of feeding yourself well. The ease of sitting down without rushing off to the next thing.

These small joys don't fix everything. They steady you.

They remind you that goodness is still finding you, even in quiet ways. Even on days when resilience feels thin and starting over felt like all you could manage.

Pay attention to what lightens your spirit just a little. Those moments matter more than you think.

<hr />

**Soul Note**

Joy doesn't have to be big to be real.

<hr />

**Soul Pause**

What small joy has found you recently?

Where have you felt a brief easing you almost overlooked?

How might you make room for these moments without demanding more of them?

<hr />

**Prayer**

God of gentle gladness,
open my eyes to the joy already near me.
Teach me to receive it without suspicion
and let it carry me forward.
Amen.

# 46

# What You Remember Shapes What You Carry

"I will remember the deeds of the Lord; yes, I will remember your miracles of long ago. I will consider all your works and meditate on all your mighty deeds." Psalm 77:11–12

Gratitude often begins as memory.

Not the polished kind we tell at gatherings, but the small, lived moments that return to us without warning. A kitchen from years ago. Hands that taught you how to measure by feel. A voice calling you to the table.

These memories shape us quietly.

At the counter, stories linger in familiar motions. The way you reach for a bowl. The recipe you make without checking the card. The comfort of doing something the same way someone once did it before you.

Gratitude isn't only about noticing what you have now. It's also about honoring what carried you here. The people. The moments. The love that showed up in ordinary forms and stayed with you.

When you remember well, you don't get stuck in the past. You gather strength from it.

You carry forward what was given to you, sometimes without realizing it, until one day you recognize it in your own hands.

**Soul Note**

Memory can be a form of gratitude when it is held gently.

**Soul Pause**

What memories return to you when you're in the kitchen or at rest?

Who taught you something that still shapes you today?

How might honoring those stories deepen your gratitude now?

**Prayer**

God of those who came before us,
thank You for the stories that shaped my life.
Help me carry them with gratitude,
and pass on what is worth remembering.
Amen.

# 47

# Where Faith Actually Shows Up

"Faith by itself, if it is not
accompanied by action, is
dead. James 2:17

Faith doesn't only live in sanctuaries.

It shows up in kitchens and waiting rooms. In hospital halls and quiet conversations. In moments no one planned for and no one would choose.

Getting cancer is never on anyone's agenda. Neither are illness, relationship strain, financial uncertainty, or sudden change. They arrive like curveballs, disrupting what we thought we knew about our lives.

When I was going through cancer, I never thought of it as a blessing. I didn't frame it as a bonding moment or search for silver linings. I was focused on getting through. On the next appointment. The next round. The next day.

But looking back, I can say this with clarity: it was a blessing.

Not because cancer is good.
But because faith showed up.

I had nurses and medical staff praying over me. I found myself praying for other patients.

My mom and I planned our family's Thanksgiving and Christmas meals together in the midst of it all. There was care. There was connection. There was presence I never would have experienced otherwise.

How many people can say a major illness became a place where faith met them so clearly?

Faith looks like praying for someone before surgery. Faith looks like making a nourishing meal to welcome a new baby. Faith looks like sitting in a waiting room with a church member while their spouse is undergoing surgery. Faith looks like walking alongside someone through divorce, not trying to fix it, just staying.

These moments may never make it into a sermon. But they shape lives.

Faith is not only what we confess.
It is how we show up when life interrupts us

**Soul Note**

Faith often lives where life feels most fragile.

**Soul Pause**

Where have you witnessed faith showing up in unexpected places?

What moments in your life revealed care you didn't know you needed?

How might you honor those experiences without needing to explain them away?

## Prayer

God who meets us everywhere,
thank You for showing up beyond the walls we expect.
Help me recognize faith when it arrives quietly,
and trust that You are present even in the unplanned places.
Amen.

# 48

# God Is Closer Than We Imagined

"Where can I go from your Spirit? Where can I flee from your presence?" Psalm 139:7

Many of us learn to look for God in specific places.

Sanctuaries. Sacred words. Moments that feel set apart and unmistakably holy.

But life has a way of expanding that understanding.

When faith shows up in kitchens and waiting rooms, something shifts. We begin to notice that God is not confined to the places we prepared in advance. God meets us where life actually unfolds.

God is present in the pause before surgery. In the meal made when words feel inadequate. In the long hours spent waiting with someone you love.

This kind of presence doesn't announce itself. It doesn't always feel dramatic or reassuring in the moment. Often, it simply stays.

And staying matters.

We don't always recognize God's nearness while we're in the middle of it. Sometimes we only see it later, when we realize we were held in ways we couldn't have orchestrated ourselves.

God's presence is not dependent on our awareness. It does not retreat when we feel overwhelmed or unsure. God is closer than we imagined. Closer than our explanations. Closer than our expectations.

Once you've seen this, it changes how you move through the world.

You begin to trust that no place is godforsaken. No moment too ordinary or too disrupted to be met with care.

**Soul Note**

God's presence is not limited to where we expect holiness to be.

**Soul Pause**

Where have you noticed God's presence in unexpected places?

How has your understanding of holiness shifted over time?

What would it mean to trust that God is already near, even now?

**Prayer**

God of nearness,
open my eyes to Your presence
in the places I least expect.
Teach me to trust that You are with me,
even when I cannot name it.
Amen.

# 49

# Living as If God Is Already Here

"He has shown you, O mortal,
what is good. And what does
the Lord require of you? To act
justly and to love mercy and to
walk humbly with your God."
Micah 6:8

When you trust that God is near, something in you softens.

You stop rushing to prove faith and start practicing presence. You listen more carefully. You move through the world with a little less fear and a little more openness.

Living as if God is already here changes how you show up for others.

You don't feel the need to fix every situation. You can sit with discomfort without trying to explain it away. You learn that being present is often more faithful than saying the right thing.

At the counter, this looks like staying instead of hurrying. Offering food without needing a reason. Letting silence be enough.

Nearness reshapes compassion.
It frees you from performance.

When you trust that God is already at work, you don't have to carry everything alone. You can join what's unfolding instead of forcing outcomes. You become attentive rather than anxious.

Living this way doesn't make life easier, but it makes it more honest. You begin to trust that God's presence goes ahead of you into every room you enter.

You're not bringing God with you.
You're noticing God already there.

**Soul Note**

Presence is a form of faith.

**Soul Pause**

How would your daily interactions change if you trusted that God is already present?

Where might you slow down and simply stay?

What would it look like to release the pressure to perform faith?

**Prayer**

God who goes before us,
help me live with awareness instead of anxiety.
Teach me to trust Your nearness
and let it shape how I love.
Amen.

# 50

# The Courage That Comes From Not Being Alone

"Keep your lives free from the
love of money and be content
with what you have, because
God has said, 'Never will I leave
you; never will I forsake you.'"
Hebrews 13:5

Courage doesn't always feel bold.

Often, it feels quiet. Like taking one more step when you'd rather stop. Like speaking honestly without knowing how it will be received. Like staying present when leaving would be easier.

This kind of courage grows when you trust that you are not alone.

When God's nearness becomes something you live from instead of think about, fear loosens its grip. You don't have to be fearless. You only have to be willing.

At the counter, courage looks like beginning again. Sharing what you've learned. Letting yourself be seen. It looks like ordinary faithfulness practiced one moment at a time. Courage doesn't rush in. It steadies.

You find yourself doing things you once avoided, not because you feel strong, but because you feel held. Trust reshapes risk. Presence makes room for honesty.

The courage that lasts is not fueled by confidence. It's sustained by companionship.

**Soul Note**

Courage grows best in the presence of trust.

**Soul Pause**

Where might you take a small, honest step today?

What fear feels lighter when you remember you are not alone?

How has trust already made you braver than you realize?

**Prayer**

God who stands with me,
give me courage rooted in Your nearness.
Help me move forward with honesty and care,
trusting that I do not walk alone.
Amen.

# 51

# The Hope That Stays

"May the God of hope fill
you with all joy and peace as
you trust in him, so that you
may overflow with hope by
the power of the Holy Spirit."
Romans 15:13

Hope doesn't always look like optimism.

Sometimes it's quieter than that. Less shiny. More patient. It doesn't promise that everything will turn out the way you want. It simply stays when things are unfinished.

This kind of hope is born out of experience. It knows disappointment. It has learned how to wait. It has survived moments when answers didn't come quickly or clearly.

At the counter, enduring hope looks like keeping familiar rhythms. Making coffee. Feeding yourself. Returning to small practices that remind you life is still unfolding.

Hope stays when the story isn't resolved.
It stays when healing takes time.
It stays when you don't know what comes next.

This is not naïve hope. It is tested hope
You don't cling to it tightly.

You let it sit beside you, steady and unassuming, reminding you that God's presence has not left, even when circumstances haven't changed.

The hope that endures doesn't shout.
It breathes.

**Soul Note**

Enduring hope is quiet, patient, and faithful.

**Soul Pause**

Where have you seen hope stay with you over time?

What practices help you remain steady when outcomes are uncertain?

How might you honor hope without forcing it to be cheerful?

**Prayer**

God of abiding hope,
thank You for hope that stays when answers delay.
Help me trust Your presence
and live faithfully in the meantime.
Amen.

# 52

# Trusting the Story as It Unfolds

"Your word is a lamp for my
feet, a light on my path."
Psalm 119:105

Most of us want the whole story before we trust it.

We want clarity. Resolution. A sense of where all of this is going and why it matters. We want the assurance that what we're living through will make sense when we reach the end.

But life rarely works that way.

More often, trust looks like a lamp left on through the night. It doesn't illuminate everything. It doesn't show you the full path ahead. It simply gives enough light to take the next step without fear.

God's presence often works like that.

You are not handed the whole story at once. You are given moments. Scenes. Chapters that unfold as you move through them. Trust grows not from knowing how it ends, but from discovering, again and again, that you are not walking in the dark alone.

At the counter, trust shows up in small continuations. You return to familiar practices. You keep feeding yourself. You keep making room for care, courage, and hope, even when you don't know what comes next.

You learn to live without demanding the ending.

Trusting the unfolding story doesn't mean everything feels good or easy. It means you believe there is light enough for today, and that tomorrow will meet you when it arrives.

The lamp stays on.
The story keeps moving.
You keep walking.

**Soul Note**

Trust doesn't require the whole story, only enough light for the next step.

**Soul Pause**

Where are you longing for certainty right now?

What might it look like to trust the next small movement instead of the final outcome?

How has light already met you along the way?

**Prayer**

God of unfolding grace,
help me trust the story as it is being written.
Give me light for this moment
and courage to take the next step.
Amen.

# Sending Epilogue: You Don't Have to Hold It All

"Come to me, all you who are
weary and burdened, and I will
give you rest." Matthew 11:28

There comes a moment when you realize how tightly you've been holding on.

Not because you wanted control, but because you cared. Because you didn't know what would happen if you loosened your grip. Because carrying everything felt safer than trusting it could be held another way.

But even strong hands grow tired.

You were never meant to hold the whole story. Not the outcomes. Not the people you love. Not the weight of what's unfinished. Some things are meant to be carried together. Some things are meant to be set down.

At the counter, you learn this slowly. You cannot stir forever. You cannot keep every dish in the air. Eventually, you step back and let heat, time, and rest do their work.

Faith invites that same release.

Letting go does not mean you stop caring. It means you trust that care does not begin and end with you. That God is at work beyond what you can manage or imagine.

And now, as you step away from these pages and back into your own ordinary rhythms, the table is not closed.

The chair remains. The invitation continues. Perhaps that is what grace looks like. Bread shared. Hands open. Nourishment received for the road ahead.

You don't have to hold it all.
You never did.

**Soul Note**

Letting go is not losing faith. It is resting in a care larger than your own.

The table remains set. The invitation remains open.

**Soul Pause**

Take one slow breath.

Imagine yourself seated at a table where nothing must be earned and nothing must be proven.

What have you been holding too tightly?

Where might release bring relief instead of loss?

What would it feel like to trust that you are not the only one carrying this?

## Sending Prayer

God who holds all things,
receive what I can no longer carry.
Bless what has been done
and tend what remains unfinished.

As I step back into my ordinary days,
help me trust that Your care goes with me.
Nourish me for the journey ahead,
and remind me that I never walk alone.
Amen.

The counter remains, and Maggie's cabinet
still holds what is needed.

# A Gift From The Counter

## Simple Communion Bread

*This simple bread is meant to be shared. May it remind you that grace is received together,*
*and nourishment is never meant to be carried alone.*

### Ingredients

- 2 cups (230 grams) whole wheat flour

- 1 cup (125 grams) white flour

- ½ cup brown sugar, packed

- ¼ cup robust molasses

- 2 egg whites

- 1 teaspoon baking soda

- ½ cup oil (canola or vegetable)

- ½ cup cold water

**Instructions**

1. Preheat oven to 350°F (175°C).

2. In a large bowl, mix all ingredients together until a soft, sticky dough forms.

3. Turn the dough onto a lightly floured surface and knead gently four to six times, just until it comes together.

4. Divide dough into four equal pieces.

5. Roll each piece to approximately ¼-inch thickness.

6. Place on a baking sheet and bake for 10–15 minutes, until set but still tender.

Serves approximately 100 people (communion portions).

*The counter is still here. Come back anytime.*

## Stay a Little Longer at the Counter

If you'd like to stay a little longer at the counter, I've shared a special gift with you.

Nannie's Sourdough Starter and Bread Recipe has been passed down through generations and carries its own stories of patience, care, and nourishment. I've included a few reflections alongside it as a thank-you for walking this journey with me.

You can receive it here:

https://daretoliveagain.com/countergift

If you'd like, I also send occasional gentle notes from the counter with reflections, updates, and new offerings. You're always welcome.

From my counter to yours, may what you make here nourish more than hunger.

— Laura

# One More Moment at the Counter

If these pages met you in a meaningful place, a brief review is a simple way to help others find their way to the counter when they need it most.

Thank you for pulling up a chair.

# Recipe Index

# Scripture Index

# About the Author

Laura Sharp-Waites is a pastoral counselor and Christian Soul Coach with a Master of Divinity in Pastoral Counseling. Her work is shaped by the belief that faith is most often formed in ordinary places—kitchens, waiting rooms, and everyday moments of care.

Through her writing, baking, and coaching, Laura invites others to slow down, tend what is weary, and notice how God meets us through simple acts of presence and nourishment. Her approach is rooted in compassion, lived experience, and hope that endures in unfinished seasons.

Laura is also the host of the *At the Counter with the Baking Pastor* podcast, where reflections on faith, life, and the kitchen continue in conversation form. When she's not writing or recording, she can usually be found tending sourdough, baking something comforting, or setting the table for whoever might need a place to rest.

*There is almost always something warm in the oven.*

www.ingramcontent.com/pod-product-compliance
Lightning Source LLC
Chambersburg PA
CBHW061431150726
47987CB00001B/177